Eliminate
Meditate
Create

How to Get What You Want in a Distracted World

Elsa Moreck

Laura, light
Travel light
&
Laugh loudly!
♡ E.M.

Noise

Some lose themselves in the noise
Others create it
But some still look for a way to shut it off
They learn to speak in silence
To ask their soul what it's hungry for
And to their surprise,
It dances them to the music

For my spine,
Rita, George, Mary, Christie, Zoe, and Maria,
My hands,
Every true friend to ever grace my space
And my heart,
Roberto

Contents

My Story: Why You're Here

"People don't care how much you know until they know how much you care."
~ Steven R. Covey

I wasn't happy much of 2016. Sometime between raving at music festivals in Amsterdam and scarfing down vegan cheeseburgers in Austin, I found myself sucked into a meaningless void. Let's rewind though. In February of 2014, I graduated college with two degrees and no clue what to do with my life. As I tiptoed over the shattered glass from my farewell party and made my way out the front door, I noticed stuff I'd forgotten to pack still lurking in my drawers. I wasn't ready to leave Lebanon. My friends wheeled me away, but my eyes remained fixed, taking in what was left of the last five years of my life.

Kicking and screaming, I boarded my flight to El Paso, Texas and moved in with my parents shortly after. I was miserable in El Paso. The brown mountains bored me, corporate life was mundane, and my co-workers dreamless. I often used my lunch breaks to stroll around the company I worked at and open all the blinds. Less than ten minutes later, an anonymous retaliator would shut them again. I pitied the zombies around me and wondered how people became so comfortable giving up their freedom. After petty complaints my coworkers made about the several extra minutes I took during my lunch breaks, I snapped. As if gritty coffee and a lack of sunshine weren't enough to break my spirit.

Over the next weeks, I did what any sensible fresh graduate would: devised an escape plan. I had one goal and it was to leave El Paso, so I researched volunteer projects around the world and gravitated towards an opportunity in Cork, Ireland. I booked a non-refundable one-way ticket to ensure I wouldn't change my mind. I worked overtime every day for a month, sold most of my wardrobe, and wrote essays for college students to make extra cash. My parents and boyfriend at the time didn't think I was serious about going. They mocked how I would starve and be homeless in Europe if I did. But every night I visualized the luscious green hills in Ireland moist with morning dew reawakening me to my love of writing. As the deadline approached, I realized I must let go of the man in my life, and the skepticism of my parents if I was ever going to make my dream happen.

After chugging every beer there is to chug in Ireland, experimenting with every psychedelic there is to try in Amsterdam, and sunbathing under every bright sky in Cannes, I returned to Texas. My frowning parents were quiet, unable to argue that starving and being homeless couldn't have been further than my actual experience in Europe. Eager to prove me wrong, they mocked my next decision to move to Austin, Texas. Again, my mother berated me about the negative *what ifs* that awaited me.

Against their best judgment, I packed a suitcase and drove nine hours to Austin and moved in with friends I'd only met twice before. With less than five hundred dollars in the bank, a car, and the generosity of my hosts, I was able to jumpstart a life in Austin within two months. I worked three jobs: ghostwriting for students, a front desk job at a hotel, and a gig at an escape room. Eventually, I made enough to move into my own place, fell in love with a Mexican musician from South Texas, and finally made time again for writing.

Soon after, I was hired at a healthcare company with a salary higher than all three of my current jobs combined. My parents were pleased to hear about the benefits of the new job, and their restored ability to mention my accomplishments to their friends. But every day I spent in that cubicle my heart sank a little more. So, I did what every young person on the brink of a quarter life does: devised another escape plan. Except this time, it wouldn't take me on a trip to Europe. This time the escape plan was permanent. It was the creation of an entirely new path for my life; one that didn't need escape plans because every day was unique. This story is how I used that plan to transform my life. I've broken it down into tangible steps for you; feel free to skip around if you like. There are no rules here. Now let's get you a life that dances you to the sound of your alarm clock in the morning. Shall we?

Declutter, Declutter, Declutter

My story is a sentiment for the stuck and uninspired. I'd like to think we never lose our way, we merely forget. And how can we not? Modern life continues to get faster and noisier, and the demands on us to conform to the ever-grasping human is so tempting. But real wealth awaits those who return home to themselves. As children, we are taught that in order to belong we must tame our authenticity under certain circumstances. In class we want to be silly and make our peers laugh because attachment is important, but then we are scolded by our teachers to stay quiet. So it begins, a journey of suppressing the quirks and desires of the true self in order to fit in with the environment around us. We see it in the majors we study, the jobs we accept, and the partners we go out with. To be aware of this, and to question it with the intention of living true to our core and no one else's, is to take charge of our destiny. But in order to reach that point, we must reassess our lives honestly and openly, and separate what no longer serves us from that which does. In other words, we gotta get real!

Our defining journey is best thought of as one of *self-rediscovery*. Though it doesn't matter what we call it, so long as we answer its call before it's too late. Come home darling, the kettle still waits on the stove. The paint is still wet. The canvas is still blank. Everything waits to be filled with your passion.

Come home,

Elsa

1. The Art of Saying No

"Everyone's time is valuable,
but not everyone values their time."
~ Elsa Moreck

On a Saturday night in 2007, a group of five girls including myself marched into the Saudi Arabian Embassy of Tokyo to attend a private party. Weeks earlier, I had met the Saudi Arabian ambassador's daughters in person after chatting with them on Myspace, and we immediately hit it off. They invited me to the party via text and told me to bring whomever I liked. My girls and I showed up with our crop tops, overly plucked eyebrows, and freshly shaven legs ready to shake our hips. An elevator ride later, we found ourselves lost in the lavish house. We followed the music and eventually found a large foreign crowd. In the corner was a long table filled with every kind of liquor a sixteen-year-old could not afford. A few drinks later, we gravitated towards a jovial group gathered around hookahs in the kitchen. Little did we know, the hookah we were smoking was laced. About two hours into the night, we were laughing and ravenously munching on party snacks over conversations about peace relations in the Middle East. To the outsider, my social life was enticing. Here I was partying at one of the swankiest houses in Tokyo with my best friends. But for me, this was just another day. I loved socializing. I was good at it too. I smelled intentions a mile away. My phone was unstoppable, and my reputation preceded me everywhere I went. But this wasn't always the case.

When I first moved to Japan in middle school, I was unsatisfied with my place on the social ladder. Though my focus should've been on school, I had one goal and that was to be extremely popular. But as I grew older and my friends started taking up more and more of my time, my mom interjected and warned me about becoming consumed by the lives of others. I wouldn't see her words come to life until about five years later. I was obtaining my degree at the time at a university in Byblos, Lebanon. My father had wanted me to study there to learn more about my heritage. But even as a Lebanese-American, I found the culture to be very confusing. The society was a lot more conservative than I was used to. Daily life was lonely. It was hard to make friends, and my family was in another country. My life spun out of control when I refused to take the antidepressants my mother prescribed me for fear of gaining weight. After all, what would become of me if I gained a few extra pounds? I couldn't afford a therapist at the time, and my university didn't have one, so I began reading and journaling as therapy instead. I slowly but surely rebuilt my life.

In doing so, I learned profound truths about myself. I had spent much of my life defining myself through the eyes of others to avoid confronting my pain. But the result was that I had no clue who I was when I was alone. I didn't know what I wanted in life, whether it was a career I wanted to pursue, a religion I wanted to follow, a partner I wanted to date, or even what I wanted for lunch that day. For how can you build an authentic life when you can't even recognize your own authenticity? As the writer Najwa Zebian explains, "we are empty inside because we build our homes inside other people, and when those people walk away, our homes walk away with them." Fortunately, no state we enter is permanent. I started to rebuild my home internally by removing toxicity from my life. I began using each painful memory as a brick. Brick after brick, my home got taller, and my pain got smaller. Now, every few months I reflect on what needs to be removed because by eliminating what doesn't work for me anymore, I can see with clarity what does. Then I use each unpleasant memory as a brick to continue building. By decluttering my life, I sharpened my focus again on what truly mattered to me.

"The Pareto Principle," also known as "The 80/20 Rule," claims that eighty percent of our output is a result of twenty percent of our input. It took time to stomach this idea because it basically meant I was wasting a lot of time getting very little done. I first learned about The 80/20 Principle in *The Four Hour Work Week* by Tim Ferriss and was immediately interested in applying it to my life. Before I dedicated myself to any task, I paused to ask myself: "will this *really* create eighty percent of my results?" If the answer was anything but a solid *yes,* I backed off. This meant I had to part with distractions like Netflix, happy hour, and social media, if I was ever going to see my dreams to fruition. As unbearable as that seemed at the time, I knew deep down that the joy from finishing a project would last longer than immediate gratification. Day by day, I cultivated The Art of Saying No by turning down life's most tedious temptations in pursuit of effectiveness. The following is a list of what I've worked endlessly to eliminate. Despite my efforts, there are moments when I relapse into old habits. But even then, I pause and reflect. I remove the poison, which is the self-judgment that arises. Then I build with the mistakes. It is an ongoing cycle, but my home continues to grow more abundantly with love and wisdom because of it.

Toxic friendships

"Toxic people attach themselves like cinder blocks tied to your ankles, then invite you for a swim in their poisoned waters."
~ John Mark Green

People either build you or kill you. There is no such thing as a neutral encounter. This didn't seem relevant when I was younger, but with age, I've come to see how unmercifully true it is. I understand that it's not always easy to identify what relationships in our life are toxic nor is it any easier to let people go. But it strikes me as odd that we think twice before making a purchase with our money, yet we're so loose with our time. The former can always be replaced, whereas the latter is gone forever. Thus, I've taken it upon myself in the past few years to identify which relationships are hurting me more than they are helping me. The way I determine this is by the way I feel when I'm around certain people. If I feel at ease, inspired, and generally positive, then I deduce that the relationship is beneficial for me. Likewise, if a person can hold conversations that stimulate me mentally, it's a relationship worth holding on to. However, if I feel anxious, nervous, or superficial around someone, then the relationship is hurting me. It's challenging to walk away from people in our lives because even though we may feel that we are not gaining anything from them, they may enjoy our company. But these relationships are one-sided and no good for us. If there's no reciprocation of energies and ideas between people, then it's not truly a bond.

When you reach a dead end in a friendship or a relationship, you need to terminate it. You don't need elaborate lies or excuses. Simply explaining you're on a different life path and no longer see eye to eye on the things that matter is sufficient. It sounds harsh, but it'll benefit everyone. You'll find your people, and they'll find theirs. You may reconnect with them in the future, but in the meantime, find people who will push you and support you.

I continue to remove people who don't add value to my life. Consequently, I'm able to give more of my time and energy to the few who matter. I don't feel spread too thin or obligated to connect with people I have little interest in being around. No matter how far you distance yourself in thought and in action, if you're around people with toxic habits and thinking patterns, you'll absorb them.

Hold on to the people who bring you joy. They may not have all the answers, but at least they can help you figure them out. People are unique, and they come and go, but what remains consistent is our need to connect. Fulfill this need with the right people.

Judgment
"Be curious, not judgmental."
~ Walt Whitman

At a party a few months back, I challenged myself to spend an hour without judging anyone I met. It was nearly impossible. At every turn, there seemed to be a conversation with someone that lent my imagination an entire backstory. When their energy was good, I was less apt to judge. But if they irked me in any way, I immediately went into overdrive with assumption. I invite you to become more aware of the voices inside your mind. While they are real, they are not true. Pause long enough to see life from another's perspective before you judge. Creatures made of stardust are not to be taken at face value. We are all more than we show, but in order to see the beauty in others, we must pause and listen. Not only will this strengthen our ability to communicate effectively with each other, but it will help us cultivate deeper connections and an overall positive view of the world. This revelation will impact our lives and those we cross paths with indefinitely.

Likewise, when we judge ourselves we create a barrier between our rationality and our vulnerability. In order to allow our rationality to work for us rather than against us, we must be curious rather than judgmental with ourselves. Every behavior serves a purpose, whether we are conscious of it or not. So instead of asking, *why do I keep doing this* in a judgmental tone, we can try asking it in a genuine way: *why do I keep doing this?* By asking this lovingly, as we would a friend, we can begin to unwrap what's *really* going on under the surface. A question I ask myself when I'm feeling overly self-conscious or insecure is, *what is it I'm believing right now?* Usually the answer falls along the line of *inadequate or unloved.* Then I probe deeper by asking, *can I offer compassion to what's going on?*

It serves us to know that our behaviors aren't always in accordance with our intentions, and that is okay. The more we can become aware of ourselves, our ticks, and the subconscious intentions behind them, the more we can influence our psychobiology and create healthier habits.

Gossip
"News travels at the speed of boredom."
~ Carlos Ruis Zafon

Nothing is benefited from gossiping. Since I have handpicked my friends, I am fortunate because they too have no interest in gossiping. Beyond it being a waste of time, gossip destroys one's character. Since most opinions are a matter of perspective, it's dangerous to degrade other people with our words. Moreover, you carry a certain kind of energy when you speak ill of other people. This energy is revealed in your character, and because of it, few will trust you. I spent my college years losing friends because I refused to give into those who gossiped around me or about me. I found them petty, and I distanced myself. Eventually, this served me well because I met some of the most interesting people I know today.

Complaining
"I will not be as those who spend the day in complaining of a headache, and the night in drinking the wine that gives it."
~ Johann Wolfgang von Goethe

I have learned from my own mishaps, that complaining wakes dormant beasts. When we encounter any situation, we first react with our thoughts. But when we give these thoughts words, we give the situation power over us. For challenges that can be handled without help from others, it is wiser to deal with them silently. Ruminating about challenges out loud, allows them to take up more space than necessary. Think about this before you share with people, and realize you have all the answers you need inside you. It takes a calm mind to resolve matters eloquently. Make it your goal to achieve this before speaking your situations into existence.

Distractions
"Social media should be an echo of your real life, not the other way around." ~ Elsa Moreck

If you thought your social media fascination was an accident, think again. "Attention fragmentation," is a carefully studied science that first gained popularity in the 1800s, when the first slot machine was built. Basically, the science involves interrupting your attention enough times that it is permanently fragmented, and you are left with a digital addiction. But now, centuries later, you don't need Vegas to develop a slot machine addiction. You have the equivalent of a slot machine in your pocket.

There are people called *attention engineers* who specialize in how the human attention works. Unsurprisingly, these engineers found many admirers in Silicon Valley. Did you know social media inventors hire attention engineers to make their platforms addictive? In fact, the mechanics of the dating app "Tinder" mirror the experience of playing slots. The

17

rapid swiping achieves an intermittent reward of connection, followed by an option to either message the potential date or "keep playing." Recently, Tinder launched a premium version that allows you to undo the accidental "not interested" swipe, which monetizes mistakes made while the user is in deep in the zone.

I too fell into the trap of social media. I was convinced that to be a writer, I needed to grow a huge following. That is not to say it's not important to have a presence online. It's necessary to be active on social media because it's a free tool to promote one's work and connect with clients. But when creating hype about the work overshadows time spent creating the work, there is a problem. And to be certain, a ton of followers means nothing unless they're engaged and willing to purchase whatever you're selling. If I was simply interested in numbers, I'd get back into modeling. There's no easier way for a woman to get attention online than with her looks.

But the niche I'm targeting appreciates quality writing. In order to achieve that for them, I need ample time offline to come to conclusions about what I want to say. I observe, analyze, ponder, record then revisit my words until they feel appropriate to share. Slowly but surely, I've become less compelled to post on impulse and more inspired to do what it takes to become a full-time writer: write.

I enjoyed moments with loved ones again, without the pressure to document everything. It doesn't always come easily, especially when the people around me are fixated with their screens. But I realize that when I grasp for my phone, what I'm actually looking for is a temporary escape. My interest in mindfulness and meditation has been with the intention to ground in the present moment. Thus, even when it feels counterintuitive, I use my willpower to limit my smartphone usage.

If you find it challenging to break your social media habits right away, here are a few tips that can help. Turn off the notifications for whichever apps distract you the most. I turned off the notifications for

Instagram, Facebook messenger, and many other apps that bombard me with notifications.

I also removed the Facebook mobile app; there's something about that malicious red number that tests my willpower. Finally, I changed the name of my *social* folder, which contains all my social apps, to *distractions*. Now each time I open it, I'm comically reminded that I am distracting myself at my own risk.

Comparisons

"The reason we struggle with insecurity is because we compare our behind the scenes with everyone else's highlight reel." ~ Gabriele Kappes

In a world where instant sharing takes nothing but a few seconds, it's easy to feel like the entire world is either vacationing in The Bahamas or graduating with a PhD in neurobiological engineering while we decay in our banal lives. Social media should be an echo of one's real life, not the other way around. I've been there, looking at everyone's numbers (you know what I'm talking about) and feeling like they're all "crushing it," as I wallow in self-induced sorrow. It's hogwash. People carefully curate profiles that represent a picture-perfect life, but that's not how life really is.

Hell, I'll be the first to admit when I look at my own profile I'm impressed. Friends call me to tell me how great I look, and to ask me about my awesome adventures. But that isn't the full picture. I usually don't wear makeup or care much for my appearance. In fact, despite the size of my closet (which I'm currently shrinking), I'm usually in leggings or sweatpants, tank tops, and the world's most comfortable shoes. As for vacations, those are a once-in-a-time deal, especially now, because I'm working my tail off to finish this book. Hence, my life isn't only what you see on my social media accounts. It goes much deeper, and I love that.

But even outside of social media, we compare ourselves. I know you've been uncomfortable at least once in the presence of someone intimidating. We wrongly assume that some people have it together because they either know something we don't or were just born extremely lucky. But the reality is no one has it all together. People who have one area of their lives figured out lack in another area. The pretty girl with the perfect boyfriend wishes she had a better career. The man with the amazing job and the fast car wishes he were more interesting. The celebrity with a zillion fans has a drug problem and sings about suicide. Of course, I'm generalizing...but you get the point. The truth is, we all have areas in our lives we want to improve in. But when we focus on each other's successes instead of our own, we drain our energy with jealousy.

Imagine running a race with your eyes fixed on the person next to you instead of the finish line. You'd most likely run awkwardly and lose or fall flat on your face because you're not paying attention. When we spend energy focusing on the progress of others, we miss out on showing up for ourselves so that we too, may succeed. Moreover, we create stories in our minds about people that may or may not be true. But the worst part is that we stay distracted from improving ourselves.

In the example of the race, if you kept your eyes on the finish line and focused on your breathing, you'd have a much better chance of winning. Our culture heavily focuses on competition, which makes it challenging to drop comparisons. But comparisons destroy us. When I meet someone who excels in an area I struggle with, I ask questions. Often, you'll find the people you compare yourself to lack in a way you didn't expect. Suddenly, it's apparent: we're all flawed humans trying our best with what we have.

Regret
"Let us turn our mistakes into lessons,
our regrets into reflections."
~ Elsa Moreck

Regret is a fight against reality. It brings suffering because it rejects the truth; we act in accordance with our emotions. Even when we rationalize, we do it emotionally. We are neutral to nothing—so there's a load of *shoulds* in store for those who ruminate on what ifs. Do all mistakes happen for a reason? It's debatable. But what's definite is the option to choose peace with a change in perception. Nothing is lost when you look for the lesson in your mistakes. Thus, aim to live not perfectly, but joyfully.

Grudges
"Forgiveness is the fragrance that the violet sheds on
the heel that has crushed it."
~ Mark Twain

The saying, f*orgive but don't forget*, holds a dangerous sentiment. While forgiving does not equate forgetting, holding on to an angry memory in fear of future betrayal is not authentic forgiveness. When we hold on to grudges, we carry the weight of other people's mistakes. When we forgive, we rid ourselves of this unnecessary burden and resume the lightness of unconditional love. When others betray us, it's almost impossible to believe they have any love or respect for us. But if we release our anger and undress our heart, we realize the tendency to do malice is present in all of us. Only when we distance ourselves from taking the follies of others personally, can we truly forgive. Though trust may never be restored, at least we can see the people who have hurt us in a better light.

Expectations

"Immature love says: I love you because I need you.
Mature love says: I need you because I love you."
~ Erich Fromm

No one owes you anything. Harsh? It's one of the most liberating truths about human attachments. We need each other to survive. But needing other people does not equate latching on to them. If we cannot find contentment within ourselves alone, we will never feel whole, nor will we be the kind of people others enjoy being around. We are individuals on separate paths that happen to intersect, and that is a *miracle*. The kindest thing anyone can give you is their time. Never take this for granted. I've ended friendships because I was unappreciated for not giving enough of my time. This is not true friendship. Companionship does not ask you to put self-actualization on hold to answer it. Friends seek to add value to your life by adding value to theirs first, so that they may have something to offer.

Another trap I've fallen into, is thinking I need to repay someone for what they've done for me, even though I didn't ask them to. Being courteous and returning a kind gesture is one thing. But feeling guilty for someone else's generosity is uncalled for. And honestly, I hesitate to call it generosity if they did it out of a motive to get something back. Live without expectations. With practice you can hone your ability to expect less and less from people until you expect nothing at all. Even when it comes to your romantic partners, the less you expect, the more they *want* to do for you. When you live this way, you become overwhelmed with the unexpected warmth around you.

Giving Up

"Rejection is what gives resilience its flavor."
~ Elsa Moreck

When a person or an opportunity push us away from them, they push us closer to ourselves. It is a necessary evil. We become softer when we've been rejected; we become more curious, more aware of the possibilities. Sometimes it has an adverse effect of making us more rigid and unavailable, but that's just a shell we use to protect the very vulnerable jelly instead.

Defining life moments come from rejection. Whether it's in a career or a relationship, it fuels us with a deep need for change. Very few things in life dramatically redirect us like rejection. I find it so powerful. I ended up in Austin because of a failed love story. Looking back at it now, I can't imagine any other outcome that fits me as well. But you never see that in the moment.

No's light fires under our asses. They force us to look inward for answers, which for some of us is terrifying. You won't win all the hearts. You won't win all the opportunities. No matter how much charm you fit in your smile. No matter how many punch lines you deliver in your pitch. Thank rejection when it slams the door in your face. Bow to it and kiss the doorknob, because I promise it'll all make sense when you take a few steps in another direction.

Extraneous Possessions

"Even Socrates, who lived a very frugal and simple life, loved to go to the market. When his students asked about this, he replied, "I love to go and see all the things I am happy without."
~ Jack Kornfield

I'm amazed at the number of items I own, not in the best way. It was daunting to move when I changed apartments. I have so much stuff that it didn't all fit in my new place, so I stored the rest in a public facility. The day I moved, my boyfriend drove a U-Haul crammed with my stuff, and I followed in my car with so many items my back mirror was blocked. At an intersection, I yielded for a few seconds, but couldn't see any cars coming from my side mirror, so I proceeded. Instantly, the blaring horn of an eighteen-wheeler carrying a load of cars honked at me. I froze in my spot. I wasn't sure how close the truck was because I couldn't see it in the mirror. It drove right past me, missing my car by less than a few inches. Everything happened in slow motion, and I froze for a few seconds afterward. Then, I drove away, brushing off the near-death experience half an hour later.

We carry this luggage in our life, physically and emotionally, and wonder why we feel overpowered by circumstance. We sit shackled in cubicles, bossed around by people who want to sabotage us because they're miserable, and for what? To buy a bunch of junk we call fashion and decorations. I stayed with my boyfriend for a few weeks until my new apartment was ready, and I was envious of his simplistic life. His belongings fit in two suitcases. Mine barely fit in a 7'5 U-Haul and a SUV, *after* I donated half of it. I've imprisoned myself because I believed I ought to have seven different pairs of the same style of shoes and six different face creams. I haven't had the energy to search for my skin creams in the unopened boxes, so I haven't put anything on my face in days. Ironically, my skin looks the best it ever has. We don't need most of what we buy, yet we compulsively and consistently convince ourselves otherwise. Of course, with the help of brainwashing advertisements and persuasive marketing schemes, that isn't too hard to do. But belongings rarely make us happier. If anything, they add to our load. I almost died because of all the unnecessary crap I own. But I learned a crucial lesson in the process. Aside of a few functional and quality items that allows us to pursue what we love and feel awesome doing it, we only need good health, people, and experiences to enrich us.

Chapter Takeaways:

1. Friends either build you or kill you...choose wisely.

2. Social media has been engineered to be addictive.

3. Possessions weigh us down, mentally and physically.

I dare you to...

- Sell or donate the items in your closet that you haven't worn in the past year. Aim to get rid of at least a quarter of your closet.

- Say no three times to three different people. Whether they ask for a favor, invite you somewhere, or just ask to talk.

- Write a hypothetical letter of forgiveness to someone who's recently upset you. What you do with the letter is up to you.

2. Enlightenment for Skeptics

"Coincidences are spiritual puns."
~ G.K. Chesterton

As a teenager, I began searching for answers to my many metaphysical questions. I grew up Catholic, but the lessons taught in church didn't resonate with me. It often felt like ideals were imposed on me without an explanation why, which I took great conflict with. Upon exploring other religions and philosophies, I discovered Buddhism. I've always appreciated Eastern philosophies because they make sense to me. There are comprehensible explanations behind their ideals.

Despite my drift from the church, I have found a harmonious connection between the monotheistic religions and the eastern philosophies I've studied. I've concluded that the commonalities are relevant enough to acknowledge a spiritual presence in our life, one beyond what we can see daily. And when this presence is embraced and understood, however that is achieved, our faith is renewed.

Our sense of belonging isn't complete without an understanding of the world as a whole. Though I do not have all the answers, and I don't ever expect to, it brings me peace to understand my part in this magnificent world. My inner self, or intuition, offers me all the knowledge I'd ever need to succeed. I can't find this knowledge in any written textbook or from any mentor. This deep-rooted inner self is tied to something beyond the material world that we experience daily. It's the feeling that warns you about a stranger or helps you decide when you're stuck between two possible outcomes. In designing my career, I've relied heavily on this feeling. I've also seen the consequences of neglecting my intuition in favor of my intellect, as people betrayed my trust, professionally and socially.

We all have access to an infinite storage of worldly wisdom, but we stray from it as we become members of a society that doesn't appreciate inner work. Instead, we focus on the external: appearance, social status, and relationships. While all three can contribute to temporary validation and happiness, we become completely dependent on external factors to experience joy. We operate automatically, responding to our subconscious wants without taking a moment to pause and reflect. The faster life gets, the crazier our impulses. But this has dire consequences on our lives and the lives of those around us. Working from the outside in, instead of the inside out, results in a society dedicated to conformity instead of authenticity, which inevitably leads to collective cognitive dissonance.

Meditation
"The affairs of the world will go on forever.
Do not delay meditation."
~ Milarepa

Each day for at least five minutes, I lay or sit in silence and focus on the sounds around me, then on my breath, until I finally reach a middle state of consciousness. I begin to feel like I am melting into my seat, fully present. Recurring thoughts come, as they always do, and I watch. At first judgmental, then with curiosity. Once I clear the way for my thoughts to pass freely without judgment, a novel one appears: this is it. This moment and everything I've invited into it.

I have learned through a consistent meditation practice that I have a deep-seated fear of letting go of the past. In a sense, the past is dead and gone, and letting go of it is accepting that. This love that I gain through silent non-judgmental contemplation brings understanding. It allows me to observe without ridiculing, which unfolds a new layer of truth each time I do it. We will all die one day. If we have nothing else in common, we have the breath we share now and the death we will eventually experience. Let us not judge ourselves in that time in between, and instead, continue to be lovingly curious.

People have stigmatized meditation for being cult-like. But the experience of meditation extends far beyond sitting cross-legged in silence, and many of us meditate without being aware of it. Personally, I meditate when I write. Writing is a way for me to shut out the world momentarily as I allow words to flow subconsciously onto the page. My life has always been very noisy. Learning to tone down the noise to focus on what matters was the goal of meditation for me. I also wanted to soothe my anxiety and learn to engage my life in the present. When I am not meditating, I increasingly work to perform one task at a time. This is difficult because I love to multitask. Sitting down for a meal is always better with an episode of my favorite show in the background. Talking on the phone is easier if I'm walking around, and the list goes on. But our brain cannot process two pieces of data at the same time. Hence, when we multitask, both tasks inevitably suffer. Despite this, I still choose to do it because it is fun and feels more effective than it actually is. The consequences of multitasking aren't as dire for the most part. However, failing to spot and control mental patterns can be.

Studies in neuroscience reveal that on average, the human mind drifts forty seven percent of the time. That's a lot. We have an average of about sixty thousand thoughts a day, ninety percent of which are repeated from the day before. Hence, you can sense just how stuck we can get in our mental loops. To break these patterns, we must actively monitor our thoughts. It doesn't need to be become an obsession. Simply bringing kind attention to recurring thoughts, and labelling them for what they are, is a great way to manage our cluttered minds. For instance, when I realize I'm consistently thinking about something I said earlier that day, I begin to label it as *repeat thought,* whenever it comes back up in my mind. Sometimes I'll even use my hand to gesture that I'm done ruminating about something. I might say aloud, *we're done with this,* then shoo my hand in the air simultaneously to signal that. It sounds a little kooky but learning to spot my habits and the tricks my mind plays on me, has played a tremendous role in making me a better thinker, and as a result, a better writer.

The Power of Thought
"Your imagination is your preview of life's coming attractions." ~ Albert Einstein

Despite my doubts, I have embraced the concept that my imagination creates a large portion of my circumstances, and this realization has dramatically impacted my life. Our experiences are a matter of imagination and perspective. Though every one of us constantly creates a different life, we all exist in the same world. Within this world, there is an abundance of resources, people, love, and kindness. Despite this, many are starving, many are lonely, and we fight over resources and land. We have the knowledge to produce clean energy, yet we stubbornly cling to environmentally cruel ways to generate more profit. And profit, an imaginary currency we created, drives most of us into directions that lead to frustration. We continue to feel small and powerless. If we fail to live up to societal standards, we're made to feel insignificant. And if we do hit all the check marks, we're likable and rewarded. We obsessively strive to meet expectations set by outside sources, hardly appreciating the miracles along the way, and never reaching our destination until it's too late to enjoy it. But it doesn't have to be that way.

The birth of an idea is like planting a tree. Once the seeds are planted in the mind, they grow into reality. Let's say you crave an ice cream. You get into your car, drive to the nearest ice cream parlor, and find yourself licking the ice cream you craved moments earlier. If you craved a house, you would eventually come to own it in the same manner. The difference between the two is that the cost of the ice cream is less; hence it's much easier to obtain than the house. From what we know about economics, this is true, but only to an extent. My experience of eating an ice cream and living in a certain house are not so different. The house I live in now was once an idea, just like the ice cream. I thought of specs I wanted, i.e.: wood floors, modern, new, close to downtown, and well within my budget. I was so desperate to find a house with these specifications, that I threw all my energy into it when I realized I was running out of time to find a place before my current lease was up. Within twenty-four hours, I signed a lease on an apartment with these exact specifications. It is important to note, that the budget I chose for my apartment (under nine hundred dollars), is unheard of in Austin. But I found it because all I thought about was securing my objectives within the time frame I had, and the idea of settling for anything less never occurred to me.

What you pay your attention to determine what your life looks like. Many people think of their thoughts and actions as two separate entities. But this is far from true. Firstly, your thoughts are not private, even if this appears to be the case. The reason the truth always surfaces is because thoughts turn into actions, and actions are visible proof of one's thoughts. Advertisers spend trillions of dollars every year injecting ideas in the minds of consumers. Do you think it's a coincidence that the most popular social media platforms eventually become ill with advertisements? Companies care deeply about your thoughts because they know how powerful they are in determining your behavior.

When it comes to creating your career, you must free yourself of skepticism with the reassurance your professional future is within your control. To some, this idea is freeing, but to others it is terrifying. If our lives are truly a product of our own creation, then we are suddenly tasked with a huge responsibility. No longer can we blame our parents, our bosses, our government, or any other outside force for our dissatisfaction. On the other hand, this responsibility also means that the sky's the limit. If we're set on seeing our objectives come to life, they will. When things don't happen the way we initially thought they would, we find out later it was in our best interest. In happier times, I remind myself to look back and appreciate my mistakes for playing a pivotal role in getting me to this point. I realize whatever happens, whether I perceive it as good or bad, continues to serve my underlying mission. Hence, my unshakable belief that destiny is a product of imagination, allows me to trust what comes my way. Tragedies are a result of individual and collective fear that has ripple effects. Unfortunately, these effects destroy individual and collective lives. It's very hard to remain positive in the face of so much global tragedy. But we have the option to use our pain as a pedestal, from which to rise above our circumstances. Lastly, we can find solace in the idea that despite what is happening in the world, we still have the power to control our destinies thereby uplifting not only our lives, but the lives of those around us. Observe, and you will arrive at this realization and feel the power of its liberation.

The Weight of Words

"The limits of my language
mean the limits of my world."
~ Ludwin Wittgenstein

When I was a little girl, I was fascinated with magic. It wasn't so much the tricks that interested me, but the boldness of the magicians convincing an audience of a reality they knew was a gimmick, but helplessly surrendered to with awe anyway. I was particularly curious about the two silly words magicians preceded their tricks with, *abra cadabra*. Why did they say it? At once ridiculous, but essential to the history of magic, I came to find that *abra cadabra* comes from the Aramaic language, (the language supposedly spoken by Jesus), and it means "what I speak, I create." How mesmerizing a discovery. As someone often in search of a balance between the spiritual and physical realm, I fell in love with the weight of these two words in the real world.

Words, whether they are thought, read, heard, or said, directly impact our lives. Hence, it is only clever to choose words carefully, even in the most casual settings. There are times when this is challenging, and as a member of organized society, I can relate. But we can choose our words wisely if we always pause to think about what to say before speaking. Omitting a few words from responses, or avoiding the tendency to make up excuses, can make us more positive and truthful with others and ourselves. Oral words, unlike written captions, cannot be edited once spoken. To master the Art of Conversation, we must pause between our thoughts, and practice active listening of others. Another way to improve speech is by replacing negative words with positive ones to trick our minds into attracting better situations. For example, I have eliminated the word 'problem' from my vocabulary. Instead, I've replaced it with the word 'challenge.' Problems reveal something negative, whereas a challenge sounds more like a puzzle...not easy, but achievable. Another word worth debunking is "failure." Though seemingly useful, this word diminishes any opportunity for looking on the bright side. By definition, failure means, "lack of success." But humans learn through trial and error, and the best entrepreneurs will you tell you if you're not failing, you're not trying. While I agree, I urge you to replace the world "failing" with "redirecting." When you refer to failures as redirections, your perception of the word changes. Suddenly, the word involves a positive concept. Excuse the idealism, but I believe failures are redirections. I've always taken away lessons from my failures, albeit a harsh way to learn, the wisdom sticks. In all sense of the word, failures are redirections. They get us back on track by pinching us when we need it most.

An example of redirection is heartbreak. I found that I learned the most profound lessons about love when I was heartbroken. I always had a skewed vision of what love was like. I treated it like a way to complete myself, and accordingly always felt and acted like half a person. It wasn't until I lost who I thought was my other half and couldn't find a suitable replacement, that I experienced wholeness and self-dependence. When I met my current partner, I was internally peaceful. Our mutual ability to find joy from within, enabled us to move at a healthy pace together and build what is now the best relationship either one of us has ever experienced.

Aside from replacing negative words, I also recommend only speaking words that align with your innermost desires. If you wish to have love, do not speak of heartbreak and misfortune. If you wish to have more money, do not speak of the lack of it. Bills are proof that you're trusted with sums or services, thus do not hate or fear them. Money is a means to an end, and it should be only seen as such. What used to be dealt with in paper is now mostly digital, which makes the transactional use of money even more illusory. Luckily for us, reduced handling of paper can be a way to forget about it and focus the mind on more important matters. If you mostly use cash, don't fret. The underlying concept is the same: money is a means to an end, there is an abundance of it, and if you demand more, it will be given. It is not selfish to demand money. If you have a negative relationship with money, it's helpful to remember that money isn't evil. It's the way in which some obtain it that is. To attract money is not to exploit others, but to receive what you deserve for your contributions. We live in an abundant universe that is strangely accommodating. So, if those around you judge your desire to attract money, then change your environment.

Constantly speak your ideal situations into existence. I let many people in my life know I was writing this book; I even told strangers. Talking about it made it feel real, and it helped me hold myself accountable to finish it. I'll be talking more about this in Chapter 6: "How to Hold Yourself Accountable."

Finally, pay attention to people who have already fulfilled your dreams. If you have friends in healthy committed relationships, observe them. I follow writers I respect on social media, and I let their situations inspire mine. This can be applied to any example, such as a woman on social media who just got married, or a man who just bought a new car. Since our universe is vast and abundant, there is no need to be competitive. If you can open yourself to be inspired by other's situations, instead of jealous, you can use their examples as fuel for your objectives.

Several months ago, I was working as a front desk agent at a local hotel in Austin. I checked in a beautiful young woman with a dark complexion and blonde hair. Upon conducting the usual small talk, I learned she was a writer. I was very intrigued. This woman, only a few years older than myself, was already a traveling full-time writer. But I wasn't jealous; I knew better. Every time I checked her social media, I felt gratitude because her life motivated me to live mine. I knew I could self-actualize and become a full-time writer if I desired it too.

Letter to Self and Vision Board
"It is a terrible thing to see but have no vision."
~ Helen Keller

What followed my interaction with this writer was a journey towards rapid self-actualization. I already had a website at that point, but I wasn't really taking my work seriously. Meeting a writer in real life who had similar demographics, amplified my motivation. Suddenly, a whole new world of opportunity opened in front of me. It's funny how moments like this happen all the time, but we don't acknowledge them. I'm glad I acknowledged that moment; otherwise, I wouldn't be here now.

A few weeks after meeting her, I created a vision board. I'd already written a detailed letter to myself before I traveled last year that discussed where I wanted to be in life the next time I read it. But I wanted a vision board to see every day and remind myself exactly where I was going. For those of you who don't know what a vision board is, it's basically just a poster with pictures of your dreams on it. I like to collect random magazines and cut out pictures that feed into the image I'm creating for my life, and then I glue them onto a white poster.

The vision board I have now contains pictures, sentiments, and quotes, about health, wealth, travel, love, and publishing. It's very powerful to see what you want before you every day. As I discussed earlier, our thoughts determine our reality, and ultimately our future. The more we can bombard our minds with images of the life we dream of, the more likely we are to have those exact dreams come true.

The Weight of Materialism
"To be content with little is difficult;
to be content with much, impossible."
~ Marie Von Ebner-Eschenbach

I realized while traveling, that having substantially less stuff made me happier. I was flexible and able to go anywhere anytime because my essentials were with me. I wish I'd adopted a minimalistic attitude earlier because I wouldn't have to spend precious time selling and donating my belongings now. But I won't dwell in regret. The lesson has been implanted in my mind and will forever impact my purchasing behavior. As I unpacked my boxes upon moving into my new apartment, an overwhelming feeling of guilt settled in. I realized my possessions had a certain kind of energy about them. I believe the items we own have mental attachments that form energies of their own. These attachments may be a recollection of the settings in which the items were obtained. While I love to look back on memories occasionally, a sense of captivity fills me when I look around my house and realize these memories no longer have any relevance to my present life. They are simply clutter. In the same manner that we must part with our past to make space for the present, we must part with old items to make room for the new.

We throw away just about the same amount of clothes that we buy, and it's easy to see why. Watch any Hollywood film and the protagonist will dawn a new outfit in almost every scene. I've already discussed the influence media has on your thoughts, thus your purchases. On the contrary, tune into a European film and you will find that the protagonist wears the same outfit for several scenes. Closets are also considerably smaller in Europe because they tend to consume less clothes! We have defaulted ourselves as the land of abundance and consumerism, but luckily there is a wave of minimalism sweeping in to change that. When you have less options, you make better choices, and the same goes for clothes. Conscious buying requires that you know where your clothes came from, and that they be good enough quality that you won't have the urge to toss them out a few months later. But this isn't a plea to convince you become a fanatic every time you reach for your wallet. It's simply a reminder to take a step back before you make a purchase and consider why you're making it. What's influencing you? Do you really need it? Is the item functional for your everyday life? Will it enhance your experience?

Materialism, like every ism, is an exploitation of materials. We do not need half the items we own, but we buy them anyway. We purchase for aesthetics, pleasure, or worse, for display. Some people are traveling across oceans with barely enough clothing to keep them alive in harsh conditions, and I have a public storage for the stuff that doesn't fit in my house. That's insane. I'm not against purchasing things. It is the overindulgence of the unnecessary that I warn against.

Minimalism is clearing the way for what really matters. We often think of protesting as taking to the streets with signs. But this is only one kind of protesting. Another kind of protesting is managing our purchasing power. We have the choice every day to choose where we spend our money. There are tangible ways to stop supporting the exploiters of our world, and to become more compassionate. It starts by learning more about what goes into the products we buy. By making wiser spending choices and caring for the items we already own, we can lead a sustainable lifestyle and set the example.

Writing this book has inspired me to become extremely sensible with my purchases. I have decluttered my house multiple times by donating and selling items I no longer use. It is not easy to part with certain things, but I understand that is only because we attach sentimental value to our belongings. To combat this, I make conscious choices to hold on to the memories while getting rid of the stuff affiliated with them. I have witnessed the refreshing sensation of a house decluttered, in which every item inside holds a purpose. This has allowed my things to be in service of me instead of the other way around. Moreover, by offering up the possessions that are idle in my life, I create an opportunity for someone else who finds them useful to benefit, and that brings me great satisfaction.

Our Relationship to Food
"If you don't love it, don't eat it,
and if you love it, savor it."~ Evelyn Tribole

My past with professional modeling compels me to write of our intricate relationship with food. I learned at an early age that what one eats bears more consequences than how much one exercises when maintaining a particular body weight. Hence, I picked up a strict calorie counting regime at the young age of thirteen. My relationship with food was very pragmatic. I allowed myself a certain amount of calories a day. So long as I remained below it, I felt good about myself. In later years, this relationship dissolved the busier I became. Thus, I'd eat when I was hungry, and forget about food when I wasn't. I gained a little bit of weight as a result, and eventually was uncomfortable with it.

During my first year in Austin, I roomed with a vegetarian and a vegan, and eventually stopped eating meat myself. I observed that on a vegan diet I was a lot less lethargic. Several months into my newly adopted vegan diet, however, other symptoms arose. I felt lightheaded often, and like meals didn't satiate me, so I'd snack more than usual. This is probably because I didn't explore the plant-based diet nearly as much as I could have. There is an array of options available to vegans that are delicious, satiating, and healthy. But I also fought against my guilt for craving fish. Between cheat days and trying to talk myself back into getting on track, my feelings about food became complex and troubling again. Meanwhile, I observed what foods sat best with my digestive track. It seemed that fish fueled me in a light way that I appreciated, and that dairy did not wreak nearly as much havoc on my stomach as gluten. Eventually, I discontinued my vegan diet, despite the benefits it has on the planet and my health. I found that I was not ready to give up fish or dairy yet, and after judging myself for a long time because of this, I still moved forward with my decision. Having said that, the vegan diet is an aspiration that I strive towards in every meal. I eat red meat sparingly, replace dairy with alternatives whenever I can, and rely mostly on fish as my source of meat. I count calories, but not in the intrusive way I did as a teenager. I am aware that eating soothes anxiety for some people. Ripping my cuticles and picking at my skin is how I soothe mine. But I am in the process of using meditation and loving awareness to break these habits too.

Nonetheless, I love to eat, and I was chubby as a child so my eating habits have always been complicated. The first modeling agency I auditioned for commented on my weight, which only exacerbated my low self-esteem. It wasn't until I decided to forfeit my modeling career altogether that I began to heal my connection to eating. I chose a profession that favored my merits instead, which allowed me more wiggle room with my weight and re-instilled the idea that my worth is not tied to my body type. I interact with food naturally now. I appreciate it for nourishing me but understand that not everything in front of me is necessarily good. I'd rather hold out on chips and eat a full meal that will satiate me, than scoff down three hundred calories in the two minutes it takes to finish a bag of Doritos. I also choose to read labels of what I buy because I like to know what goes into my body. Being conscious of how I eat is not merely vanity as it is a mindful way to take care of this body I call home. That being said, I do not scrutinize myself or others for eating meat. Regardless of the impact it has on the planet, we have been doing it for centuries and shaming each other is not the way to inspire change. If you are a vegan, a vegetarian, or aspiring to be either, understand that you are only responsible for your dietary choices. Furthermore, there is extensive research showing that the majority of American vegans and vegetarians eventually return to eating meat. When we are prevented from something, we only crave it more. Thus, in order to make progress towards eating a healthier diet with less animal products, the way isn't through fear, shame, or guilt. For most people, decreasing their intake of meat proves more effective than eliminating it altogether. Through awareness that we want to treat our bodies and our planet well, we can decrease the amount of animal products we eat. On the same note, we can love and appreciate our meals even when they contain animal products. We can hold the memory of those who suffered to nourish us with tenderness. We can slow down and chew our food properly to savor every flavor in our mouths. We can share a meal with people we care about, and bond over sustenance. We can heal our relationship with food, and with our bodies, one bite at a time.

Chapter takeaways:

1. Meditation is training the mind to focus on a task continually without interruption.

2. Words are more powerful than you think; use them consciously.

3. Minimalism is buying what is functional in everyday life, and it clears the path for creation, physically and mentally.

I dare you to...

• Write a detailed letter addressed to you, about what you dream of your life looking like in three years. Let your ideas roam free.

• Be as creative and detailed as you want. List the people you're around, the country or state you live in, the way your home looks and feels, and the work you do every day. Truly describe the life you desire if limits didn't exist, and you could have it all.

• Date the letter, put it in your wallet, then read it once a year, on the same date you wrote it if you can.

3. Hustle like You Mean It

"Create before you consume."
~ Marie Forleo

There was a deep sense of guilt when I first quit my job a few months back. I didn't feel bad because I regretted my decision, but when I freed my time, much of it was wasted doing little of value. Thomas Friedman, an American Journalist, speaks of the troubles that arise for those who secure "freedom from, but not freedom to." What he means is that many people walk away from something they do not want, but not towards something they do want.

When I was working at my old job, I thought what held me back from writing was a lack of time. What I discovered soon after was that a lack of time was not it. It was the lack of meaningful work. The difference between meaningless and meaningful work is that meaningless work does not excite you. Every day is redundant, filled with tedious tasks that you find boring and useless. When you're faced with such a bland reality, it's challenging to create anything of value.

I didn't know this when I quit my job because I was bored and sluggish. I was writing, but not with zest. Finally, my boyfriend told me about an opening for a position to tutor seventh grade English at a public middle school here in Austin, Texas. I was slow to react. I didn't know if I wanted to add yet another obligation to my plate. I already had a book to work on and an extensive ghostwriting project. Nonetheless, I emailed my resume and immediately followed it up with a call to the recruiter. A week later I was hired.

My life has shifted since. It has been the most rewarding and humbling experience to interact with students daily and make them better at what I love: writing. Moreover, the relationship I have with each one of them continues to deeply enrich my life.

All the pressure I had to organize my time has disappeared. I inherently know what to do with it now. Creating, socializing, and relaxing, fall where they naturally should without overthinking it.

A good career enables us to use our intuitive skills to get results for other people. I discovered early on in my career that I was not as motivated by money as I was by meaning. In the past, I convinced myself that wanting a job I liked was selfish. It seemed like everyone I talked to hated their job, so who was I to like mine? I continued this self-sabotaging cycle for two years until I finally realized that my increasing salary was not increasing my happiness.

Our system is broken. We teach our children obedience and humility instead of effectiveness and creativity. Thus, we're brainwashed into believing that life is a series of checklists. You finish school and go to college where you sit and listen to people talk for another four years at your own expense. Then, just when you think you've reached the finish line, you find yourself in a cubicle listening to people until the day you reach retirement. At which point, your bones are brittle from spending your life in a seat, and your sense of adventure has been reduced over the years to corporate slavery. We deal with all this bureaucratic crap all day long, from shuffling papers to attending useless meetings where half of the room is disengaged, and the other half is on a power trip. Adults that have nothing in common aside from their love for money spend precious moments of their lives faking small talk and scarfing down fast food in thirty minutes in front of three monitors. It's a reality many of us can relate to. But even when we acknowledge how monotonous it is, we still feel trapped, because we find comfort in the fact that at the very least, this reality is predictable. Changing course scares the hell out of us.

What will we do with bills? What about our resume? I fully empathize with the fear that comes with leaving a job. But you only find answers to an alternate reality when you believe in one. If you believe your life should be spent performing a set of meaningless duties, and answering to people you genuinely disagree with, then your fate will be as such. But, if you have ever pondered other ideas that could possibly be a source of income one day, then you've already taken the first step.

"But I don't have any good ideas," the inner critic might say. The average human has about sixty thousand thoughts in just one day! Even if you don't care to be an entrepreneur, you still might have ideas of things you'd rather be doing with your time. Perhaps you want to bake gluten free desserts for a living or paint. Whatever it is, there is a way in our modern world to monetize it. We forget that many innovators were once like us...caught up in the tedious plights of everyday life. But what distinguished them from the clear majority was their willingness to act on their ideas. All of us have great ideas, and the only factor standing between us, and our ability to turn our ideas into sustainable careers, is our willingness to pursue them.

First things first, write down your ideas. I have hundreds of pages of Google docs filled with my ideas. I love using Google docs because it's free, and you never lose anything on the Cloud. I've also set it to work offline, so even when I'm on a flight and I get a stupendous idea, I can record it. Once you have your ideas down, the next step is to decide which of them deserves focus. Let's be real, just because we have a lot of ideas doesn't mean they're all good. But even if one of those thousands of ideas is worth your time, you'd have to take it seriously to find out.

You may need a business plan. Business plans are important because they require you to think about your idea critically and to do research to predict your success. You can find business plans online. Their formats may differ a little, but generally, they all ask for the same information. I created a business plan for both my writing and my ghostwriting work. Doing so helped me understand my niche in both markets, and to target accordingly. It also saved me a lot of money on advertising when it came to my ghostwriting company because I realized that word of mouth was stronger than my online efforts. Thus, instead of pouring money into social media ads, I created a loyalty and referral program for my existing clients.

Once you've completed your business plan, which may take a few weeks or even months, depending on your business idea, the next step is to establish an online presence. I set up my website in less than ten minutes with a YouTube tutorial. First, I bought a domain name from Namecheap (www.namecheap.com). Then, I chose WordPress (www.wordpress.com) to set up my actual website because you can endlessly customize it. But there are many other websites that make it much easier to design your site for a small cost every month. Examples are Weebly (www.weebly.com) and Squarespace (www.squarespace.com). Both have extremely user-friendly platforms and excellent customer service. Unless you're a coder or have a budget to spend on frills, I discourage you to use Wordpress. You will constantly have to update your plugins and protect your site because there are more security concerns with the way WordPress is set up. You will also need to learn at least some HTML and CSS to keep your website up to par, which will distract you from your professional objectives. Otherwise, you will need to hire a designer which I will discuss shortly.

Finally, I chose HostGator (www.hostgator.com) as the host for my website. I recommend using Bluehost (www.bluehost.com) instead of HostGator. I've heard from word of mouth that they have much better customer service than HostGator. If you buy your domain through Weebly or Squarespace, you'll skip this step altogether because they provide their own hosting services.

If you're absolutely set on creating a highly customizable website and don't mind splurging on designers, feel free to use WordPress instead of the suggested alternatives. The advantage of using WordPress, is that you will never be limited to using the provided templates, which is the case on websites like Squarespace and Weebly. Designers from all over the world create plugins and templates that you can integrate into your site. This also means that you will be able to create a unique website that you can always add to. But you may have to purchase a paid theme to get the look you want or pay a designer like I mentioned previously.

If you decide to work with a designer, use the tips I'm about to give you and save yourself time, money, and stress. Moreover, these steps can be used when hiring any freelancer, not just a website designer.

1. ***Find someone credible to do the job.***
   A credible person should have a website for themselves, and an impressive portfolio with at least five websites designed in their name. If the developer you're considering doesn't have a personal website that blows your mind, what are the chances they can create one that will blow yours? Would you trust a dentist with yellow teeth, or an overweight dietician? Think about that.

2. ***Create a contract.***
   This is very important, because if anything goes wrong this is your only way of fixing it. I am telling you this from my own experience. I outsourced my website to a group of developers who installed an incomplete theme which didn't function properly. But there was nothing I could do about it. After all was said and done, they had my money, and it was my word against theirs. I ended up having to hire another designer to pay for their mistakes. In

the case that you hire a freelancer without using a third-party service like Thumbtack or Upwork, create a contract. There needs to be clear guidelines on the services you're paying for, otherwise it is impossible to hold the people you hire legally liable. I'm not encouraging you to expect the worst, but when it comes to investing time and money in strangers, it's better to be safe than sorry. Outside of business, *trust* people until they give you reason not to. But in business, *doubt* people until they give you reason you not to. I learned that the hard way in the freelance world. For pre-made contract templates, check out Docracy (www.docracy.com). This a free service used by attorneys that will meet most of your freelance contract needs. *This by no means replaces legal advice from a lawyer or an attorney.*

3. ***Only pay a minimal fee upfront and get an invoice for that amount.***
The invoice is your only proof of payment. Never pay the entire amount upfront. This demotivates the person giving you the service and puts them in a position where they can screw you over (unless of course, they signed a *contract).* In my ghostwriting business, I have been paid upfront for my services. I do not ask for it, but some clients like to pay in full and be done with it. Luckily for them, this has no effect on my work ethic. But the same cannot be said for everyone. Some people would rather hustle you for some money than preserve their reputation in business. It's a sad reality and it will surely come back to slap them in the face, but there's no reason you should be a part of it.

4. ***Know the person you're hiring.***
What I would give to go back in time with this bit of wisdom. People put their best faces forward when you take out the check book. Unfortunately, it's only after you begin to work with them that you learn about their work ethic. I once hired a guy who openly told me that he worked on my projects during his train ride to work. I was very frustrated. I was paying him a lot of money and he clearly didn't value the quality of the work he was giving me. No one should treat their clients like that. *Clients* are the reason a business exists in the first place, and they deserve that respect. If you're hiring someone, have multiple conversations with multiple freelancers. Examine how they respond; are they detailed and professional? Have them present their portfolio and samples before you pay them a dime. Trust me. This isn't meant to demean anyone; I'm a freelancer too. But there are a few feelings worse than realizing your impulsive behavior cost you a lot of money and time, yet still didn't yield the results you wanted. I know what it feels like to be excited in the beginning stages and not have a clue where to begin. But don't hire the first freelancer you meet. Don't hire the second or the third either. Talk to at least five to seven freelancers, then decide. Remember, you are adding someone to your team and that takes time...time you will later save when you don't have to look for someone else.

In case you were wondering what the hell I'm talking about with all these Internet terms, don't worry. I was once as aloof as the best of us. Let me explain: A **domain** is the address of your house, it's where you tell people to go when they visit you, e.g.:

www.elsamoreck.com (my website). The **platform** you choose to create your site with, e.g.: WordPress, Squarespace, Weebly, etc...is like a furniture store. It's what you use to design your house. Finally, your **hosting site** is your house; it's where all the furniture resides.

Make sure to have a social media presence, but don't become obsessed with it. When I first started sharing my writing online, I became overly involved with my image as a writer. This robbed me of valuable time I could've spent writing. It doesn't matter how many followers you have, or how many people like your posts. Seriously, whatever business you're in, focus on delivering quality products and/or services consistently. That's your only task. Don't pay attention to the social media hype; half of it is unaccounted for. My ghostwriting company has a hundred followers on Instagram and about the same on Facebook. I haven't been active on either for more than two years, and I already have more work than I can handle due to word of mouth and returning clients. My personal writing has a bigger following, but I'm still more concerned about writing than I am about growing a social media following.

In the beginning of your business launch, you might have to work on things that may not be as fun as the personal projects you're passionate about. "Hustling like you mean it," entails doing whatever it takes to secure the freedom to do what you are excited about. I eliminated the corporate job that blocked my creativity but also took on a full-time job, and a freelance project, that weren't exactly what I had in mind. Nonetheless, both tasks challenge me and use my intuitive skills to their best ability, which allows me to stay creative as I work on my own projects. It's not merely enough to get out of an unpleasant situation; success is when you secure a more pleasant position. If you're unhappy in a relationship, end it to secure your freedom to love again. If you're discontent in your job, end it to secure work you're happy doing. If you need a break in between, take one. I took a four-month sabbatical two years ago, when I quit my job at a financial firm, and I started a ghostwriting company to sustain it.

Your goals might change over time. What I wanted for myself a year ago is not what I want for myself now. Focus on one short-term goal at a time. I usually give myself no more than ninety days to achieve a goal, because if I give myself much more than that, I lose the momentum I need to achieve it. I gave myself three months to write this book. Thus far, my tight deadline has kept me accountable to finishing it, which means I'm not wasting a day.

Finally, it doesn't matter how important others find your goals. It only matters that you care, because that's when you make them happen. Many people thought I was crazy because I wanted to walk away from a steady job to travel. I was told I would starve in Europe because of the inflation and cost of living. I was told that Couchsurfing was dangerous, (it can be if you don't trust your gut) and that staying with strangers was one of the stupidest things a person could do in a foreign country. In fact, during my layover in Scotland, I was interrogated at customs and almost not allowed to board my next flight because I didn't know the address I was staying at in Ireland. I was told employers would never look at me again after I returned with a gap on my resume. I was told so many things that never happened because I was so focused on traveling that it didn't matter. Other challenges I didn't anticipate came about during my trip, but I handled them all with courage because I trusted in what I wanted.

I started my ghostwriting company before traveling almost by accident. I helped my friend with an essay as a favor, and he offered to pay me. He was so satisfied with his grade that he asked me if he could refer some of his friends. I readily agreed thinking it'd be an easy way to make money abroad. One thing led to another, and suddenly, I found myself scheduling work calls and negotiating my rates with several clients. It was invigorating. Never, had I thought of myself as an entrepreneur. I don't even recall knowing what the word meant up until very recently. But there was an inner stubbornness that compelled me to resist a mundane life dictated by the whims of others. It was this disappointment, that led to a breakdown, followed by a breakthrough.

In four months, I traveled to three countries, wrote a book I still might publish one day, and had more adventures than some do in an entire lifetime, all due to a firm belief in "another way." I believe we give the world our best when we do what we enjoy and are naturally good at. While we may get frustrated at times, we pick ourselves up when we trust in the process of work we love. Whether you want to be a chef, code websites, sing, or knit sweaters, you can do it and make good money from it. It may not play out exactly the way you envision it, but you'll do well because when you do what brings you joy, others find value in it.

Chapter Takeaways:

1. Secure your freedom from an unpleasant situation to a pleasant one.

2. When there's less free time to squander, you become more productive.

3. Your best work is that which comes naturally to you and gets others results.

I dare you to...

Write down your career goal on a notecard, like this:

I will become a _____,
*who*_____.

e.g.: I will become a writer, who inspires others to live their truth.

Whatever your career goal is, write it down...the crazier, the better.

Put the note card under your pillow. Read it each morning when you wake up, and in the evening, before you fall asleep.

4. Demand and You Shall Receive

"Some people never get what they want because they're too afraid to ask." ~ Madonna

Not enough is said on the power of assertion. I hear a lot about adjusting expectations to reality, but hardly enough about adjusting reality to expectations. I learned early on not to waste time asking for what I know I deserve, but to demand it instead. There are times when bigger forces ask that we surrender. In those moments, it is wise to let go. However, there are situations we can mend to our making. Knowing the difference between the two is a consequence of honing our ability to live in presence. Once we are clear then, that an outcome is not permanent, we can use conscious control to take charge of it.

In these cases, I'll usually have my mind set on an outcome, and I make damn sure it happens no matter what. This expectation has transferred from one category to the next in my life. I am regularly encountered by people my age who are dissatisfied with their current situation, whether it be in a relationship, a job, their health, etc. I've realized that many people willingly play a victim role in the stage of life. But by assuming this role, you remain in character. Victims aren't ready to assert themselves to get what they want. Instead, they'd rather be told what to do and go along with whatever is chosen for them.

When you demand something, you skip the step of asking for it. Thus, there is no space for rejection. Note that you must be intuitive and sensible about your demands. For example, I would not walk into Whole Foods and demand a cheaper price on blueberries. That's stupid; I know that it's an international company and the cashiers and managers have no power over the prices of goods. Alternatively, I would not walk into American Apparel and try and negotiate the price of a scarf. Again, I would be asking for something the employees don't have the power to grant me. I would, however, walk into a leasing office of an apartment complex and convince the staff to waive the application fee on an apartment I was interested in applying for if I agreed to sign within 48 hours. Fifteen minutes into a leasing office, smiles and small talk later, there is a common likability factor that is more likely to influence them to waive the fee for me. Moreover, they're thinking I'll be pleasant to do business with in the future, and that their boss will be glad they got me to sign so quickly. I'm thinking these are the people who are going to prioritize my maintenance requests, and hey, I just saved a hundred bucks on an application fee for an apartment I already knew I wanted.

Flexibility in the Workplace
"The funny thing about rules is that they're created by humans. The funny thing about humans is that they change their minds."
~ Elsa Moreck

When I worked in the corporate world, I always found out what made my supervisor happy and focused on giving as much of that as I could. In return, I demanded flexibility. I did this at my jobs out of college, both of which were Fortune 500 companies. My peers were bitter because I was given extra privileges. But what they failed to realize was that I demanded each one of those privileges myself, often without words.

At the end of the day, your boss has a boss, who has a boss. If you work at a big company like I did, chances are their mission boils down to this: profit. If you're showing up to an eight-hour shift and completing work in an effective way, they don't give a damn how you do it. Sure, there are micromanaging bosses who will take every measure to taunt you despite how successful you are. But I quit jobs with bosses like that. For the most part, your boss is concerned with how productive you are, because productivity equals profit, which equals a happy thriving company.

Thus, do not get caught up in the mediocrities of your co-workers if you wish to have freedom at work. I used to finish more work in three hours than my peers did during their eight-hour shift plus overtime. I'm not a genius. But if you read chapter one, then you have a solid idea of the types of habits I avoid, which free my energy to focus on what really matters.

On a typical day, I'd get to the office, soothed after a nice drive, and ramped up on caffeine. I'd plug in my headphones and get to work. Once finished, I did whatever the hell I wanted and no one ever questioned me. When the phone rang, I was kind, patient, and professional. I let the customer vent if he or she was angry, and professionally responded the best way I could. In meetings, I maintained eye contact with speakers, even when I wanted to poke my eyes out, and I kept my phone out of sight. I also participated, so people in the room noticed and remembered me. Confidence goes a long way in the professional world. Much like high school, you must display your confidence to be respected.

Finally, I dressed to impress every day. I don't care how under-slept or hungover I felt. I have a few blazers, pant suits, and pencil skirts that I wore interchangeably. I kept my hair and nails neat and wore clean and well-conditioned shoes. When you look put together, even you if you feel like dying inside, you're perceived as capable and worthy of privileges. And for goodness sakes, remember people's names! If your memory is terrible, write their names down. Addressing people by their name makes them feel special. I don't need to tell you how that relates to demanding what you want in the workplace. So, make it a point to greet people using their names as often as you can, with a genuine smile and interest.

If you're an entrepreneur, all the same rules apply. If you expect your clients to take you seriously, you must take yourself seriously first. I send my clients

Google calendar invites before we have a virtual meeting, and I always maintain a formal tone both in verbal and in written communication. I had a client once ask me if I was this robotic in my personal life. But I'm not so much robotic as I am assertive and direct. I don't like small talk in work, and frankly, I hate making the time for it. To avoid small talk, I usually ask people "what's up" instead of "how are you" when I'm in a setting where I don't feel like chatting. "How are you" opens the doors of formality, and there's no telling when they'll be closed again, whereas "what's up" gets to the root of the need. It's basically asking, "what do you need from me," politely.

We all want to be treated like adults in the workplace, and when we're not, it's either because we've been plagued with petty bosses, or we don't demand the respect we deserve. While the concept of demanding respect may seem simple, it is counterintuitive to many. As children, we were taught to take orders at home and in school, but this plays against us in the workplace. People don't want to babysit you. They want to trust you'll get the job done when they turn their back, and that you'll make them look good in front of their bosses. If you do that, you're golden.

No rule is ever set in stone. If you can establish a good standing at work, meaning you do your job professionally and positively, you can enjoy a playing field of freedom. Whether you want to work from home, take longer lunches, or leave early on Fridays, your wish shall be granted if you demand it. Keep in mind that people hesitate more when you ask for a request than when you just demand it. The former requires a decision, which means they must ask their supervisors...and we all know how much people love being put in that position. If you take initiative to grant yourself freedom you know you deserve, you remove this pressure entirely. And if you're truly performing at a high level, chances are your boss will let you have that freedom anyway. If you're still denied simple freedoms despite your efforts, it may be time for a serious self-assessment. Do you value your paycheck over your freedom? While we all have responsibilities, it is important to remember that we cause everyone a disservice when we do work that makes us miserable. At the very least, we can reach a compromise in our current positions by presenting those in authority with thoughtful reasons about how flexibility can make us well rounded and more productive.

Demanding and Negotiating Money
"Let us never negotiate out of fear.
But let us never fear to negotiate."
~ John F. Kennedy

When demanding a quote from a client, remember, it is your services that are being sought after in the exchange. Never allow yourself to look desperate when interacting with a client. If they smell even the slightest hint of insecurity, they will pounce on you like a lion and impose their never-ending demands. Instead, always come from a place of calmness and expertise. If they ask for a request that was not mentioned in your initial agreement, kindly suggest that this request will require more of your time, which will take you away from other projects. Accordingly, you will need to charge more.

Set standards for your interactions. Do not let clients harass you. I have three email accounts, one personal, one for my ghostwriting company, and one for my work as an author. I only give my ghostwriting clients the second email. Sometimes I give international clients my number, but even then, it is immediately established that I respond best to email and that I prefer all requests in writing. When we do speak, I usually have a very specific piece of information I need from them. Make sure you know exactly what you need from your clients before you contact them. Like you, they are busy. You deflate your professionalism when your thoughts appeared scattered and your questions open-ended. Instead, always lead conversations with the thought of what you need in mind. Get what you need, disappear, and don't contact them again until you have the finished product.

Negotiating is an art form. Often demanding and negotiating go hand in hand. The concept of negotiating is simple, but the execution is not always as easy. Unlike demanding, negotiating means that the request as demanded was not granted, and a compromise needs to be reached. Hence, all parties involved must benefit equally for a solution to be reached. To negotiate effectively, you first need to be aware of the opposite party's intentions. When I negotiate with clients, I understand that they usually want quality work, for a minimal cost, and with the least amount of work done on their part. I study clients before negotiating. If they are more concerned with the quality of writing than the price, I share samples of my work and provide testimonials. I also continue to work with them until they're satisfied with the product, but I charge accordingly.

If they're more concerned with pricing, I explain why and how I price things and offer them suggestions that fit within their budget. I always emphasize the simplicity of the process beforehand, and I also find out why they're asking for my help in the first place. When I do this, I put their mind at ease by letting them know they're dealing with someone who genuinely cares. And I do care about my clients. I understand that like me, they're trying to prove themselves professionally in a competitive world.

Conversely, if I'm negotiating with a professional for a service I need, I always know what I'm willing to pay beforehand. By having a mental note of this, I'm able to maintain a confident tone. I usually find out how much the service normally costs and set my target quote at a twenty-five percent discounted rate.

However, since I am driven by quality, I don't mind splurging on someone who's highly skilled. Since I run a business, I know when someone hassles me for a price I find is fair, I'm apt to perform less than I would for those who value my time. Hence, I like to keep the people I do business with happy. When I show them I'm willing to pay for quality work, they give me what I want when I want it.

Choices make you powerful when you negotiate, whether you are on the demanding or receiving end. When negotiating a salary for a new job, you'll feel more confident if you have another opportunity lined up. But sometimes, you may not have another opportunity. In these cases, you must first decide how qualified you are for the position. Many of us feel under-qualified for opportunities we like, even though that is not the case. Be mindful of this, because it is important in negotiating the salary you want. Remember the company you've applied for has chosen you for a reason. If they went through the trouble to ask you for an interview, meet you, and offer you the position, then chances are you're ranking high on their likability list. It is crucial to negotiate your salary beforehand even if they mention a fixed amount. Negotiating a salary is your first raise and a chance to show your new employers what you think you're worth. It's always easier to ask for what you want before you start doing the job, so be sure to capitalize on that moment. Highlight the parts of your resume verbally and explain how your experience and expertise will be of great value to the company, and how you'd be willing to share it for X amount. I've negotiated salaries at every job I've had out of college, and I always received the amount I asked for.

Choices are important even when you're hiring someone for their services. If I want a book cover designed, for example, and there are ten people willing to do it, then I'm in a powerful position to negotiate. The same is true in reverse. If someone seeks your services and you have multiple clients, you're in a better position to demand the quotes you want.

Finally, when demanding or negotiating, keep one magical word in mind: "because." The word "because" has been scientifically proven to act as a trigger word for a "yes" response. When you provide a reason for your request, no matter how obvious the reason is, people are prone to accept. For example, "It's going to cost you $70.00 *because* it requires extra research before I can write it for you." I haven't really given extensive knowledge in my explanation, but the fact that I provided a reason is enough to make a client sympathetic to my request. If I were to negotiate a rate I want with a professional, I might say: "My budget is $150 *because* that is all I can afford." Again, I haven't really given a supported argument for my request. But going the extra step to provide a reason at all, is often sufficient.

Marry the Moment

"The meeting of two eternities, the past and future...is precisely the present moment."
~ Henry David Thoreau

How you do one thing is how you do all things. While it was noble to walk away from jobs I'd outgrown in the past, I had a tendency to grow bitter until the day I left. It finally dawned upon me that I was doing myself a disservice by constantly living in the future. Rather than fixate on leaving, I decided to experiment with the time I had left. To my amusement, I began enjoying aspects of my jobs I'd overlooked before. Personal conversations with peers or little kids in the lobby put a hammock smile on my face. I began jamming on the drive to work again; I even found an alternate route to cruise on. Phone calls with clients became more meaningful. Instead of picking up the phone begrudgingly, I became intentional about genuinely answering clients' concerns. I tapped into a world of human connection I'd previously missed out on. Ironically, when I put more effort into my job, I came home in the evening with more momentum to write.

If you are in a transitional phase in your life, set an intention to embrace the time you have left by fully committing to the present. While it is transformative to move on, it is just as enriching to

60

engage the moments we are in. It is only when we fully surrender to what's going on *now* that we can fully appreciate what comes *later*. For the past, the present, and the future, are but one long continuum of moments strung together by the illusory feeling of linear time. Thus, the present is at once the past and the future. What we put into our lives in this moment becomes a part of the whole that makes up our future.

Receive

"Until we can receive with an open heart, we're never really giving with an open heart. When we attach judgment to receiving help, we knowingly or unknowingly attach judgment to giving help."
~ Brené Brown

We are taught the importance of giving, but hardly ever the importance of receiving. When we feel worthy, we tune into the ebb and flow of true giving. It is brave to hold another's care without feeling an anxiousness to immediately return the favor. This is a practice that can be honed over time if it doesn't come naturally. We can start by becoming mindful of how we thank people. Think back to the last time you were at a restaurant. Did you feel compelled to thank the server every time they filled your cup with water or fulfilled a request? Of the times you thanked them, how many were genuine, and how many merely a conditioned social response? Put this way, how often did you match your gratitude with eye contact to truly show your appreciation? It is the mask of unworthiness that drives us to overcompensate when people are kind to us.

I have taught myself to be more open to kindness. When a friend takes valuable time to console me, I allow myself to revel in their attention. I talk as long as I need to feel restored again. It's not always comfortable, and sometimes I go on awkward tangents that in the moment feel like clutter. But it is healing to let your authenticity spill. It allows you the space to fully be yourself.

Contrarily, when a client accepts a rate I quote them, I do not overcompensate. I understand our cooperation is mutually beneficial. When a company offers me the salary I negotiated for, I accept it politely then thank them with the results of my work. Receiving is an art form. The beauty is, the more we allow ourselves to receive, the more we have to give.

Chapter Takeaways:

1. Demanding, while counterintuitive, gets you what you deserve.

2. People take you seriously when you take yourself seriously.

3. Gratitude is when you accept kindness without questioning the generosity of others.

I dare you to...

- Tell your supervisor you're planning to take a longer lunch this week. Mention that you're caught up on your work and would like to take a fifteen-minute walk after lunch to digest your meal and improve your health.

- The next time someone invites you to anything, only respond with "thank you" once. Make eye contact when you do, and lock your eyes for a while to express your genuine gratitude.

5. Resilience versus Resistance

"Most people will choose unhappiness
over uncertainty." ~ Tim Ferriss

Two years ago, I was tanning on the beach in Cannes, France shortly after taking a stroll on The Promenade de la Croisette and munching on a beignet aux pommes (apple doughnut). Weeks before that, I was rotting in a cubicle with mindless work. My decision to travel around Europe was based on absurd assumptions. I didn't have nearly as much money as I needed to stay afloat in such an expensive continent, nor did I have an extensive plan of any kind. Against the sound judgment of my parents, I boarded a plane to Ireland with a one-way ticket.

I realize this trip, along with other decisions I've made, prove how much faith I have in uncertainty, and how horrible I am at planning. Though, if I may be frank, the reason I am horrible at planning is because I don't fully believe in it. I love the spontaneity of life, the magic of the unknown. Plans always change, but when you have a solid vision, it doesn't matter what happens to your plans. They can be turned upside down but the vision will still come to life if you believe in it. But I wasn't always this confident. A few days after I quit my job to write, I couldn't help but think I made one of the dumbest decisions in my life. Because of this fear, I attracted conversations that contradicted everything I believed in. I was distraught. What had I done? Before I drowned in doubt, I recalled my decision to quit my job last year to travel. Suddenly, milestones from my trip brought back an abundance of reassurance. I remembered how scared I was to quit my job, and how worried I was that everything my parents warned me about would come true. I remembered trusting nothing but my instinct and pondering how stupid it was to do so. But somewhere in my naivety, a deep-rooted feeling guided me throughout my entire journey...my intuition. Had I not trusted it, I wouldn't have had the adventure of a lifetime, nor would I be writing this book.

Still, there was little idea as to exactly what I would do financially once I quit my job this time. The usual, *I might be homeless,* thoughts interrupted my day with panic attacks. My two-week notice turned into a draft that was just sitting in my inbox building up the courage to be sent. One day I even found myself writing down reasons why I should keep the job. I saw it as fuel for my passion because it paid for all the things I needed for my business, like a website and business cards. But there was a darker reality lingering behind my apparent rationality, a four-letter word we all know too well. So, I postponed and planned, and then I postponed and planned a little more. Until one day, I decided enough was enough. I truly studied the "worst case scenario" of being jobless, which included the consequences of temporarily living without health insurance, being evicted from my apartment, and having to admit failure to my parents, which was probably the worst of all three. Though the outcomes weren't pleasant to consider, they didn't make me falter from my decision to quit. I don't have a family to support, which helps, but I find this isn't what keeps most unhappy people in their jobs. It's the fear of failure. Fear stifles us, and the *what ifs* are enough to drive the best of us mad. Some successful entrepreneurs warn against quitting your day job before you have your business off the ground with a stable income. This advice seems a little bizarre to me, especially when you dig deeper into their own stories. Many of them quit their well-paying jobs to pick up anything that made them an income as they worked on their businesses. Marie Forleo, one of the world's most respected life coaches, quit a prestigious job working for a magazine to become a bartender, where she met many of her later clients. I think the ability to embrace the unknown, allows us to be courageous and creative. I recommend taking the leap with three backup plans...just to sleep better at night.

Here are what mine looked like:

Plan 1: Live with boyfriend until book is published, spend from savings.

Plan 2: Lease apartment under $900, and use savings to cover rent for next three months. Work part-time at a cafe during the day time for daily spending income. Live minimally.

Plan 3: Move back in with parents and live off savings until book is published. Pick up part-time job if needed.

Which one of these plans did I end up using? Brace yourself...*none*. What ended up happening looked a little more like this:

I quit my job and moved in with a friend, who was going through a hard time and needed comfort. I was very unproductive and distracted with my newly created free time. I spent most days waking up late, bonding with my friend (which was undeniably fun), and procrastinating instead of writing. Several days after guilt set in, and little progress was made on my book, I was hired to tutor English at a local public school. This quickly became the most fulfilling job I've ever had. I wrote every day and made fascinating progress on my book because of my new inspiring gig. I had enough money to move into my own place, and miraculously found a dazzling one-bedroom apartment near downtown for less than nine hundred dollars, which is unheard of in Austin. Shortly after, I booked a client for a well-paid ghostwriting project. I no longer end up working as a barista or having to move in with anyone.

That's a prime example of why I hate planning. I always thought of my anti-planning mindset as a weakness. While everyone around me anxiously planned the next years of their lives, I enjoyed the present and admitted I had no clue what I would do in the future. When the question, "where do you see yourself in the next five years?" crept up in interviews, my blood pressure spiked as I stuttered my way to a deceitful answer. I hated that damn question. Why do I need to know? Why does it matter? I have no clue what I'll want in five years if I'm even alive that long. I think I'll want to be a well-established writer. But who knows? I may pick up another passion or have an experience that completely alters my destiny. Wait, we have a word for that in English, fickle. Ah...how the meaning of that word tormented me. Being born to type-A parents didn't do me any justice either. But this entire journey has been a compilation of middle fingers in the air to everyone and everything that ever made me doubtful about chasing my dreams. So, sorry fickleness, but the middle finger applies to you too. Screw plans. Create a vision.

The difference between a plan and a vision is that a plan assumes what's coming. A vision, on the other hand, has a destination in mind but keeps you flexible to the possibility of change along the way. If my plan is to quit my job, then do x, y, and z, I might be disappointed if x, y, or z, don't play out the way I'd hoped. But if I have the vision to quit my job and become a writer, regardless of the *how* I'll succeed at doing it. It doesn't matter if I do y, then x, then z, because either way, I'm still moving towards my destination.

Short-Term Goals
"Goals are dreams with deadlines."
~ Fortune cookie

This isn't to say you shouldn't stick to one project for the sake of jumping around and trying everything. We don't want to become jacks-of-all-trades but masters at nothing. This is where short-term goals come in handy. I believe in setting one short-term goal at a time. My goal now is to write, and publish, so that's what I'm focused on. If I indulge in the dreadful "fickleness" previously mentioned, then yes, I will ultimately continue to move in a lateral direction...never truly advancing in anything. So, while your vision may still be a little open-ended, create a specific goal for every three-month period of your life along the way. Be specific with your short-term goals. *In the next three months, I will self-publish a nonfiction book,* is an example of a specific, and detailed goal that really doesn't allow much room for confusion. If I have three months to self-publish a nonfiction book, the *how* suddenly answers itself. I clearly need to learn how to self-publish first, and how to write a nonfiction book. The resources are plentiful, from books to articles, and other authors I can pull information from. That's why it's important to clearly identify my short-term goals. Once I know what they are, I can synthesize the resources to find exactly what I need. All the while, I keep myself open and flexible to change while holding my vision in the highest esteem. When I was in between apartments, I had to write from my boyfriend's bachelor pad, which traded a living room for a recording studio...hardly a conducive working environment. But when you have a specific end-goal in mind, external factors hardly affect your ability to find ways to make it work.

If you thought self-actualization was a concession of predictable events, think again. Whether you want to become a rapper, or simply want to travel the world, you'll never be able to predict exactly what's coming, good or bad. So, enjoy the journey you're on, and welcome surprises with open arms. If it's a good surprise, you'll be grateful you wouldn't have experienced it otherwise. And if it's a bad surprise; you'll gain a lesson that'll continue to serve you on your journey. Either way, you made the leap! Congratulations, you officially have more courage than half the world's population.

Chapter Takeaways:

1. Plans always change; visions are more sustainable.

2. Worst-case scenarios never happen.

3. When you truly believe in what you want, miracles occur.

I dare you to...

- Write the worst-case scenario of the risk you're considering, and what you will do about it if it happens.

- Include why you want to take this risk, and the good that'll come from it if things go your way.

- Fold the paper, put in your wallet. Forget about it, and take the risk you've been avoiding.

6. How to Hold Yourself Accountable

*"I long to accomplish a great and noble task, but it is
my chief duty to accomplish small tasks as if they
were great and noble."*
~ Helen Keller

How do you finish what you've started when
the results of your work are completely unknown to
you? Moreover, why would you commit so much time
to a project that may never amount to anything, when
instead you could be out tasting the deliciousness of
life? It's challenging for me to tackle these questions,
which gives me more reason to. I believe that finishing
a project requires that it be more ambitious than you
can easily imagine. When I started a blog, it was
exciting, but it was expected. Most modern writers
have blogs; it's the thing to do. But the project wasn't
big enough...I read blogs when I'm stuck on an issue
and need a quick fix, but I read books when I want to
enhance my perspective on life. I wanted to be the
house people invested in. That's not to say blogs are
not valuable—but for me, personally, writing books
has always been the dream. Blogs simply don't get
discussed over Moscow mules the way good books do.
      So how do you hold yourself accountable? You
create a vision bigger than yourself, and you become
accountable to it because it needs you. There is no one
that can bring to life your ideas the way you can.
What's the point of buying the seeds if you're not going
to plant them and tend to them? Yes, sometimes you
won't feel like doing it, but you just do. If you don't
water your flowers, they'll die. If you don't water your
ideas, they'll perish too.

Here are *five* rules of thumb to help keep you disciplined:

1. ***Practice your craft every day.***
   If you can put in 15 minutes of work a day, it will eventually become 30, and then an hour. There are days when you'll work longer, and that's great. And there are other days when you'll try everything in your power to avoid working on your project. That's when you need to work the most. I didn't feel like writing today. I procrastinated in the most creative ways to justify my behavior. Alas, an hour after I should've been asleep, I'm sitting in bed tapping away at my keyboard.

2. ***Tell people about it.***
   I told everyone about this book. Whether it was a friend I'd known for years or a person I just met, I found an opportune moment to mention I was writing a book. Naturally, I was asked when I would be publishing it, and without hesitation, I responded March 2017. By making public what I was doing, not only did I receive positive feedback and motivation, but I was held with public accountability.

3. ***Create a deadline.***
   I gave myself three months to finish this book and shared that deadline with the world. Tight deadlines force us to work smarter, and to work, period. When a deadline feels open-ended or far away, we continue to procrastinate.

4. ***Take your work seriously.***
   It doesn't matter if you have a day job. If you truly expect anything to come out of your talent, and you should, then it must take

precedence over other areas in your life. I devotedly agree in balance, but I also believe in hustling like you mean it. Part of hustling like you mean it involves becoming an expert at your craft. When you feel uninspired and distracted, remind yourself of the bigger picture.

5. ***Visualize the win.***
   Imagine that you are asked to give a talk about your work, interviews, and much more. What would it feel like to influence the world with a developed concept born from your mind? When you remind yourself of the true vision at hand, you will quickly become re-motivated. Finally, let your mortality be a piercing reminder of the value of time. While minute-to-minute it's easy to forget the proximity of our final hour, we approach our last breath with each exhale. Respect yourself enough to be accountable and become a master at your craft.

Chapter takeaways:

1. Practice your craft every day, even if it's for fifteen minutes.

2. Give yourself a deadline to finish your project.

3. Make your deadline public.

I dare you to...

• Write down ideas for a project you've wanted to work on. It can be to write a book, or start a podcast, for example.

• Set a deadline for three months, and make it public by telling seven different people that you'll be finished with the project three months from the date you start.

• Write down this date in your planner, on your fridge, and anywhere else you'll see it regularly. If you have social media, announce the project, and when it will be public.

7. Love like a Kid

*"This fire that we call Loving is too strong for human
minds. But just right for human souls."*
~ Aberjhani

The reason it's easy to love children is
because they don't change who they are or judge
others. You don't see three-year-olds worrying about
what others think of them or discriminating against
other children. It's freeing to be around people
comfortable with who they are because they make you
feel comfortable about who you are too. People are at
the core of any business and being talented doesn't
excuse you from working hand in hand with them. It
doesn't matter what line of work you're in, if you can't
relate to the people in your surroundings, you'll hinder
your professional and personal success. With all that's
happening in the media, sometimes it's easy to forget
that statistics we hear about refer to human beings.
We develop anger and hatred towards people we
barely know, including politicians, and people with
different socioeconomic and cultural backgrounds,
even peers we work with daily. I know what it's like to
live in a country tormented by bad politics. I'm
Lebanese, and though I didn't spend most of my life
there, I'm very aware of the corruption that has
destroyed my homeland.

Practicing Acceptance
*"I can disagree with your opinion, it turns out, but I
can't disagree with your experience."*
~ Krista Tippett

I spent my childhood in Japan, where I
attended an American High School with international
students mainly from countries around Southeast
Asia. I was the only Middle Eastern girl at my school,
and the horrifying terrorist attacks of September 11th

tarnished my country's reputation. My classmates found innovative ways to isolate me and agonize my situation. Though most of their remarks were ignorant and completely inaccurate, I let them get away with their behavior. I intuitively knew it would end someday, and that I would feel included. Soon enough, I was warmly welcomed by a group of friends who are still part of my squad today.

Though I was bullied throughout elementary and middle school, I don't remember ever feeling bitter about the experience until much later in life. Perhaps being so young made me adaptable. I grew accustomed to the culture in Japan; it naturally became a part of who I am. I loved how my parents let me walk everywhere because Japan is such a safe country. I often took the train to Tokyo on the weekends to party, or simply to shop around. Shibuya's busy streets filled with ant-like crowds navigating their way through the day, cautious not to bump into each other. Japanese people are quiet, humble, and incredibly kind. Their impeccable attention to detail never seized to amaze me. I could almost taste it as I salivated over cleverly packaged Japanese snacks while strolling through Tokyo. On the trains, the Japanese make it their mission to take as less space as possible. I often watched as a woman squeezed herself in a tiny corner of a train seat with all her belongings resting on her lap and between her feet. No one utters a word on the train. Everyone is glued to their smartphones, which were available in Japan light years before the rest of the world. Japan was home to me, even though my curvy frame, frizzy hair, and long nose, clearly distinguished me as a foreigner. I learned a lot from the Japanese, mainly how to take less space for myself to make more space for others.

After I graduated high school, I moved to Lebanon for college. Though I'm Lebanese, Lebanon didn't feel nearly like home as Japan had. College brought with it a different kind of harassment. Though I handled it with more courage as an adolescent than I had as a child, it still hurt. In Lebanon, a woman's life revolves around her reputation. Girls learn early on to be very secretive about their affairs and suspicious with their friendships. Since I tend to be transparent and friendly, I was screwed. I ruined my reputation early on in college. I didn't act different than the average college student would, but unlike girls at my school, I was honest about it. I didn't feel like I needed to hide my intentions because I never had to in the past. Eventually, I found my crowd. My sense of belonging became stronger, even though I was still an outcast in general Lebanese society. I learned to appreciate the Lebanese people, despite their judgments and social intricacies. I fell in love with my country somewhere between my second and third year of college. I lived in Byblos, a little city in Southern Lebanon, also the oldest city in the world. As I trotted down Byblos' pebbled paths towards the calming beach shores, taking in whiffs of fresh fish in my nostrils, sensations of peace restored my unbalanced college life.

Upon graduating college three years ago, I moved to El Paso, Texas. I was yet again thrown into a new world of adventures. I quickly picked up the Spanish language in the year I spent there. When I quit my first corporate job to travel, I moved to Europe. I started my trip in Cork, Ireland, one of the oldest villages in the country. I was engulfed by the generosity and sanguinity of the Irish people. I stood out with my dark skin and brown hair and was more welcomed because of it. I spent the rest of my Euro trip in Amsterdam. There, I had a familiar feeling when I observed how people shrunk themselves to make room for others on the tram. I learned to appreciate how unapologetically blunt and funny the Dutch people are, and how customer service doesn't exist since waiters don't count on receiving tips.

I moved to Austin, Texas soon after leaving Amsterdam. It was easier for me to adjust since I was born American and had attended American schools abroad. But even though I was already familiar with the culture, it took time to feel like I was a part of it.

Within a few months, I made some friends at work and began to create a social life here. Suddenly, I felt profound wisdom come from all my international experiences. Anywhere was home when I opened my heart to its people and accepted their differences.

Inside out Approach to Conflict
"Standing each by his monster, they looked at each other, and smiled."
~ E.M. Forster

For the majority of my life, my motivation to become better came from a lack of being enough. In high school and in college, I worked out and dolled up in an attempt to be validated for my beauty. As I grew older, I gradually began to shave off the idea that I had to lead with my looks for respect. But I only did so after replacing it with an equally destructive perspective: I have to become successful to be loved.

As an adult, I started seeking love I already had by thinking I needed a best-selling book to define me first. Was it an attempt to hide behind success because I don't feel worthy unless the label author comes before my name? I'd forgotten everything else that made me human. Like when drums roll and my hips shake that I feel as alive as when my fingers dance on the keyboard. I forgot that I live to experience presence in the people I encounter moment to moment. I forgot my place as a daughter, a sister, a friend, a lover, but mostly, I forgot who I am beneath it all. We are not our titles.

I can blame social conditioning endlessly for the reason we feel we are in the first place. What if you don't ever live up to outside expectations, or worse, your own? I had to face this reality recently. But I had to do it without judgment. We must love ourselves through our flaws if we wish to outgrow them. This unconditional love brings understanding. It allows us to observe without ridicule, which unfolds new layers of truth.

We live like protagonists of a conflicted story. Stumbling and falling, we fight in the attempt to achieve a dramatic climax and reach the other end. And though we're only the center of our lives, we're not alone. We may bond over troubles in passing, but many of us rarely take deeper looks into each other's lives. When we accept that everyone else is suffering too, it becomes possible to love those who cause us pain. Loving doesn't mean you need to hang out or even talk. The simple feeling of wishing someone well is enough to heal.

If you're having trouble with another person, look for the pain instead of the viciousness. Focus on their eyes the next time you speak and try to imagine what they've gone through to harden them this way. No one is born wicked. We start out life sincerely but learn defense mechanisms along the way to protect us when our vulnerability is abused. When you learn to forgive yourself with every breathe, you become more receptive to forgiving others. People begin to treat you differently. This has done wonders for my career. I've seen co-workers and clients transform, simply because I decide to look at them differently. I am fascinated by humans and our many brilliant facets. When people ask me how I know that everyone has more layers than they show, I tell them to undress their soul more often. For it is only in sharing our own vulnerability that we can invite others to be truthful in our presence.

It's simple but not easy to do this. I'll be the first to admit that sometimes people I barely know rub me the wrong way. It might be that a girl flirts with my boyfriend in front of me, or a man tries to outwit me with exaggerations. But I try and remind myself that all of us are insecure and carry weight from those insecurities in our interactions with each other. While I may not agree with another's behavior, I can empathize with our mutual need to be accepted and appreciated. We learn as we get older, that in order to be accepted and loved, we have to live up to certain standards. In time, we adapt those expectations as our own and forget what it's like to simply be as we are. To love like a kid is to overcome that and rediscover yourself. I find the notion of self-discovery dangerous because it implies an outer journey. When in truth, we disconnect with ourselves when we struggle to belong to the outer world. Indeed, reconnecting to our true selves is what we all long for; it is our highest human aspiration. The beauty of this undertaking is that it has ripple effects. We can live as open as children again, and life's beauty can be restored in its simplicity. The possibility is always present.

Chapter Takeaways:

1. Wherever you are now is home.

2. Love yourself simply for being; it's your birthright.

3. When you change how you see others, they treat you differently.

I dare you to...

- Think of someone you have a conflict with. Instead of seeing the situation from your perspective, put yourself in their shoes.

- Write down what you think their life might have been as a kid. What makes them this way? Who, or what, in their life makes it challenging for them to feel loved as they are?

- The next time you interact with this person, smile for no reason. If they treat you in a discomforting way, pause before you react. Remember they come from pain just like you.

- Recall what you've written about them and allow them to be. See if anything changes with how you perceive each other moving forward.

8. Build an Empire and Inspire

*"So what are these barriers that keep people from
reaching anywhere near their real potential?
The answer to that can be found in another question,
and that's this: Which is the most universal human
characteristic - fear or laziness?"*
~ Richard Linklater: Waking Life

The day I quit my second corporate job, my
co-workers praised me as I was gathering my
belongings before heading out the building. I couldn't
understand why they admired me, when they too, had
as much freedom to walk away as I did. I know we like
to believe our responsibilities and duties to others hold
us back, but it is not so. We hold ourselves back
because we fear change and failure. But the more we
hold ourselves back from living, the more reluctant we
are to admit we ever had an alternate dream for our
lives. Settling becomes our new reality. Situations we
invite seem to be bad cards we've been dealt. When we
pass up the opportunity to take our lives in the
direction we want, we give that responsibility to
someone else. We sit in the passenger's seat, watching
as our life is driven by the whims of those we believe
oversee us. It is impossible to taste the sweetness of
life when we are consumed with the idea that our
situation is a result of bad luck or circumstance. And
though it is excruciating to accept the possibility that
we've chosen this life for ourselves, it's the first step to
transformation. We no longer let our race, gender,
parents, history, trauma, or memories define us. It is
not our fault that we have some of the traits and habits
that we do. But as adults, we have the choice to stop
letting the inner wounded child determine what our
lives will look like. We have the power to rule over our
destiny with thoughtful awareness.

Many of the dreamers I met in the past,
profoundly inspired me to believe in my crazy ideas

enough to pursue them. My heart has been torn apart by such dreamers...artists who follow their dreams to no end. But I know now, that I met these people not to share a deep involvement with them, but with myself. They inspired me to take the road that led back to my heart. Before, I led a quiet life of conformity. When my parents didn't allow me to pursue writing as a career, I took a conventional path which led to dissatisfaction. On this path, I met people who only appreciated me for what I had to offer externally. I kept my words private in journals, and even when I thought to share them, the people I'd let into my life seldom appreciated them.

The more I learned to replace a wanting to be accepted, with a wanting to be, the more joy I experienced. To be wasn't sitting in an office because it made my parents happy. To be wasn't dating a man I had little in common with simply because everyone else liked him for me. To be wasn't lying to myself about who I was, simply because I felt like I needed to fit a certain mold. To be wasn't to inflate my ego with excess pleasure and materialism.

To be is to pursue my life's work, which is to make others confident enough to pursue their life's work. To be is to love unconditionally those who've hurt me. To be is to let go of the past, and fully immerse myself in the present. To be is to forgive me for my flaws, and still, find myself adorable despite them. To be is to forgive others and see them in a better light when they need it most. To be is to listen to my friends and family without judging.

You can be the person who inspires others to do what they're dying to. Building an empire requires living true to you. It means sitting down and honestly asking, what do I like? What excites me? What do I really want from my life? After having these answers, it becomes our responsibility to include them in our experience. But perhaps the beautiful thing in all of this is that we are not alone in our wanting. Everyone wants to be happy, loved, and fulfilled. My hope is that you will live true to yourself. The biggest regret people have in old age is sacrificing their happiness for others. And even those who expect a lot from us secretly wish to live for themselves too. After years of disagreeing with me, my mother wept when I told her I was in the final stages of my book. She explained how she'd spent her entire life pleasing others, and that seeing me stubbornly cling to my dreams made her realize how much she regrets not living a life of her own choosing.

When I left both corporate jobs, I watched as my bosses, men older than I, cheered me on. It's a funny feeling to go against the grain of societal approval only to be congratulated for it. This is what I call *purposeful nonconformity*. When you are truly authentic, being unique is effortless. People mistakenly believe that if they are true to themselves, they will lead a selfish life. On the contrary, the best version of you does the best for the world. An uninspired you, means living at half of your potential and giving the world a quarter of what you could otherwise. Unfortunately, sometimes we feel like our authentic self will not be appreciated. I know this feeling all too well. Having been raised in a predominantly scientific family, I always felt like the outsider...and a failure at that. But I had to completely let go of all the notions of success that had been shoved down my throat since I was a child and look at my life as an objective viewer. Who am I? I asked myself all the same questions I asked you in this book. When I realized I was a person who lives to create, and appreciates meaning, spontaneity, and adventure, I decided it was time for a radical change. Radical comes from the Latin word, *radicalis*, which means *forming the root*. In a sense, I was forming my roots, by becoming who I truly am. As I began to peel off the layers of conformity one by one, I felt an enormous weight lifted. I blossomed into my liberated self, and to my surprise, watched as the world made a special place for it.

The Power in Presence

"The only way to live is by accepting each minute as an unrepeatable miracle."
~ Jack Kornfield

It's humbling to inspire others with your life, and it doesn't take a writer to do it. All it takes is a person with courage. Courage is what compelled you to grab this book. Somewhere along the way, you figured the words of a sensible dreamer could inspire you, and here you are. I know what it's like to have doubt and be doubted. But risks aren't riskier when you're older, you just become more aware of the consequences. In other words, it's always easier to jump when you're a little naive about all the possible outcomes. My naivety is what enabled me to enjoy a sabbatical in Europe. Fear for my safety and professional future wasn't enough to keep me from going. This was nearly three years ago. While I appreciate that I'm older and wiser now, I stubbornly cling to that young fearlessness. To combat complacency, I often rewire my self-talk to that of a supporting friend, who acknowledges consequences, but isn't paralyzed by them. It's impossible to improve your life without change, and it's impossible to change without taking risks. Nothing is as scary as realizing you didn't take full advantage of your life. Regardless of your beliefs in an afterlife, you owe it to yourself to make the best of this life while you're here. Every day won't be as good as the next, and some people are more light-hearted than others. I've suffered from anxiety and depression since I was a teenager, and I continue to work towards overcoming both. When I find myself leaning into the dark, I visit with friends I haven't seen in a while. Gazing in the eyes of those who care about you is enough to remind you of your good nature. While it's easy to take those closest to us for granted, we must remember that like us, they are ever changing. The person you kissed this morning on her way to work, is not that same person returning to you in the evening. We're always evolving, always trying our best with what we have. During all the chasing and building, we must pause to ask if the path we're on is truly *ours*, and not one laid out by someone else for us. If we walk a path that's not aligned with who we are, we risk wasting our lives in pursuit of a disappointing destination.

Modern life is safer and more superficial. Crime is the lowest it's been in decades. As a species, we are more accepting towards each other. But there's a caveat: it's easier to stay stuck in trance. We have the world at our fingertips. Now more than ever in history, we are encouraged to practice mindfulness in our relationship with technology. We cannot create anything great without periods of deep concentration. Distraction, as we know, is the nemesis of that.

Financial instability, competition, global warming, and job insecurity, are also realities of modern life. The goal of presence is not to remain passive in the face of these realities, but instead to become adept at overcoming them. Modern neuroscience reveals that a quiet mind is optimal for mental health and steady attention. Responsibility is made of two words: response-ability. You have the *ability* to *respond* however you choose, and that is free will.

Viktor Frankl explains it best, "between stimulus and response there is a space. In that space is our power to choose our response. In our response lies our growth and our freedom." Use the pause between stimulus and response to claim your power and take ownership of your destiny.

Know Yourself

"To know yourself as the Being underneath the thinker, the stillness underneath the mental noise, the love and joy underneath the pain, is freedom, salvation, enlightenment."
~ Eckhart Tolle

Get to know yourself. Sit in silence. Start your day out with a tea and meditation ritual instead of scrolling through social media. Take more deep breaths and fewer pills. Drink more water and less alcohol. Smile more than you pout. Seclusion, is not the same as solitary. Seclusion is what we feel when we are uncomfortable in our isolation. In the company of others, we express ourselves. In our own company, we construct ourselves. A balance of both is necessary to lead a whole life. It takes a great deal of effort to be comfortable alone, especially if you are not particularly an introvert. Solitary is enjoying one's own company while still feeling connected to a larger whole. Uncomfortable answers to desperate questions we've asked sometimes only arrive if there is no one around but us to greet them. Thoughts need physical space to roam. The silence inspires them to come out and talk to us openly. Truth after truth, we unfold the layers. A sense of freedom fills us when we allow ourselves to sink into the questions, deeper and deeper, letting go of our grip.

Show up as a hundred percent you in every exchange, whether it's an interview or a date. Showing up as yourself means you *trust yourself enough to do that*. Trusting yourself means *you're confident enough to do that*. Employers and partners want confidence; they want you. When you know yourself well, risks feel more like taking the advice you'd give a friend than leaping into a fire pit. Grandiose plans become achievable goals, and dreams become realities. I wasted so much time trying to figure out who I was through the eyes of other people, frantically looking for answers in all the wrong places. Don't do that. People wonder how someone who looks so whole can be so broken, but what they don't see is the glue that holds them together. A thousand compliments don't stick with us nearly as much as one cruel remark does. But we cannot expect external validation to make us feel whole. What we can count on is our determination to heal, to work from the inside out.

The first step to healing is to learn how to be alone with ourselves, and at peace in that aloneness. For how can you get to know someone unless you spend quality time with them? If others are worthy of our friendship, shouldn't we be worthy of it too? It is in this aloneness that we discover how we truly think. The more we learn how we think, the more we can expect transformation to take place. Healing comes in many forms; music, laughter, and writing are examples of healthy outlets for pain. Unfortunately, for some of us healing is sought after with remedies that only offer temporary relief and long-term destruction, such as alcohol, drugs, or meaningless sex. Despite what we do to deal with our pain, the inevitable truth is that we all experience it. To run away from pain does not make it go away. Nor does it help to judge ourselves for it. No one is above pain. And no one is too cool to feel. While some may carry themselves as such, deep down, they too experience pain that they have not worked through. This shows itself as contradictions in their speech and behavior, and in their inexplicable need to inflict pain on others. Until we face our pain, (and we will all be forced to at some point), we cannot evade roadblocks that stand in the way of our peace. Depression comes from the Latin word *depressio* which means *push down*. Many of us navigate our lives feeling heavy because we've pushed down our pain and left it there.

Name It to Tame It
"Man's task is to become conscious of the contents
that press upward from the unconscious."
~ Carl Jung

To heal, we mustn't identify our thoughts and actions as good or bad. Instead, we are encouraged to observe objectively and forgive ourselves for them. If you are prone to self-bashing, it's going to take practice, patience, and trust, to offer yourself self-forgiveness. When you surrender, and allow yourself to be—flaws and all, you begin to find their source. You realize not all behavior is intentional, and that most of what we do comes from a deeper place we've ignored.

Have you ever watched an exorcism movie where the character was possessed? Did you notice how the priest extracts the evil spirit by calling it out by its name? The demon weakens when the priest addresses it directly. It works the same way with our negative thoughts and patterns. The moment we can acknowledge them, simply by naming them, they begin to loosen their grip over us. Become real with yourself, but above all, non-judgmental and unconditionally loving. We have all had our fair share of suffering, which directly contributes to the negative patterns we display. We do not need to inflict more pain by being cruel and self-judgmental. The more we can forgive ourselves, the more effective we can be at improving in every area of life that we wish to.

Risk
"Only those who will risk going too far can possibly
find out how far one can go."
~ T. S. Eliot

You don't need anyone to validate your choices for you. Learn to trust the screaming voice inside who urges you to take leaps of faith to get to the next point in your life. The truth is, it's hardly the risk anyone is afraid of, but the calamitous possibilities that arise from taking it. We're not afraid to fall in love; we're afraid of heartbreak and rejection. We're not afraid to jump off a cliff; we're afraid to fall and break a limb. We're not afraid to ask for a raise; we're afraid we don't qualify for it. We're not afraid to quit our jobs; we're afraid we'll be homeless if we do. But once you jump, you quickly realize the fall is nothing like you pictured it. We land more gracefully than we think, we become wiser from the heartaches, and the jobs we quit never come back to haunt us. While we cannot completely predict what lies ahead, we can certainly imagine it, which is half the work. But failing to take risks for fear of consequences that are entirely imagined is nothing short of placing an irremovable block in your path. The unfortunate thing about your thoughts is that you and only you can choose them. Since your life is a result of your thoughts, no one can fix your circumstances without your full cooperation. Imagine what can be before you see the evidence, for that is how all of advancement occurs. Risk like you live once. Risk like your contributions to this world matter. Risk like others have a reason to look up to you. Risk like your life depends on it because it does darling, it does.

When we talk of falling prey to grasping, it is not to be confused with manifesting potential. There is a difference between living greatness and feeding a deficiency. The former implies we are already enough but seek to self-actualize because it allows us more room to grow and inspire. The latter suggests we are not where we need to be yet to be loved. Our best self is our true self. That is the primary goal of self-actualization. To reconnect with what's been lost and rediscover the beauty that we already are through a mastery of mind, body, and soul. We do not aim to correct—we aim to connect.

I want you to try an activity. Read the directions first, then attempt it. Close your eyes. Now, imagine the end goal. What is the dream? Where would you want to be if there was a fairy that could grant you the wish without any strings attached? Forget the possible roadblocks; focus on the dream. Feel it with all your senses. What are you wearing? Feel the garments of your outfit. Whose hand are you holding? Is it soft or a little coarse? How big is the crowd you're speaking in front of? What is their reaction when you come on stage? What do you when you wake up in the morning as the person you dream to be? With your eyes still closed, cultivate that vision in your mind.

Hold on to that vision, and smile. Open your eyes. I know you're not living in the dream you just created *yet*. But stay true to it. Keep that vision vivid by revisiting it every week, even for a few minutes. You've planted a seed, and it will come to life. Allow it to grow. But rest assured, it is coming. When you plant a tree, do you dig up the soil everyday just to make sure it's growing? No. You water it and trust that it will bear fruit one day. I speak of the same concept with our visions. Act as if though you're already the person you dreamed up, because you are.

Epilogue

When I first published this book last year, I was tutoring English to seventh graders at a local school in Austin, Texas. Since then, I have mastered my Spanish and now work as a trilingual life coach at a charter school, empowering students from all over the world to blaze their own trails. I am also working on a second book about the sexual taboo in Lebanon. In it I expand on the gender segregation in Lebanese society, the virginity paradox, purity culture, and fixation with female physical beauty. I study the impact of these issues on one's relationship with sex. With the tools I share in this book, I've been able to hone my writing discipline and expect to publish my second book in the next few months.

Another recent fascination of mine has been studying the personas we project, be it online or in person. When I first published *Eliminate, Meditate, Create,* I became preoccupied with getting the word out about it online, understandably. But what resulted was a deep introspection into the ways in which the Internet has re-defined how we interact and present ourselves to the world. Modern standards have pushed us into hyper-superficiality, escapism, and an inhibited openness to reality as we know it.

I've been analyzing my persona and asking myself: How do I want people to see me, and what do I do to come off that way? By often checking in, I close the gap between self-enhancement and authenticity. So long as we lose ourselves in a character, we cannot be fully present. Learning to surrender is a path I am keen to share because it offers the choice to live lighter. As frustrating as the process can be, it is our greatest purpose, from which our unique gifts are born. The noise isn't easy to tune out but challenging ourselves to the task is the journey that taps us into our highest potential.

Presence

When the moment calls

And you finally hear the water pound

Like angry falls

Pause

Don't follow the sound

Let it come to you

Stay still, little one

What's in your head isn't real

Even when it feels true

This moment, right here

Don't force it

Let it come to you

ADDITIONAL INFORMATION:

Drop a line at hello@elsamoreck.com

You can also learn more about my work at
www.elsamoreck.com

If you enjoyed this book *please* rate and review it on Amazon. With your help, I can spread the word of this book and future works!

You can find it by searching for
Eliminate, Meditate, Create on Amazon.
Thank you for your support!